LEARNING IN THE FAST LANE

8 WAYS TO PUT *ALL* STUDENTS ON THE ROAD TO ACADEMIC SUCCESS

SUZY PEPPER ROLLINS

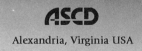

Alexandria, Virginia USA

1703 N. Beauregard St. • Alexandria, VA 22311-1714 USA
Phone: 800-933-2723 or 703-578-9600 • Fax: 703-575-5400
Website: www.ascd.org • E-mail: member@ascd.org
Author guidelines: www.ascd.org/write

Gene R. Carter, *Executive Director;* Richard Papale, *Acting Chief Program Development Officer;*
Stefani Roth, *Interim Publisher and Acquisitions Editor;* Julie Houtz, *Director, Book Editing & Production;*
Miriam Goldstein, *Editor;* Georgia Park, *Senior Graphic Designer;* Mike Kalyan, *Manager, Production
Services;* Cynthia Stock, *Production Designer;* Kyle Steichen, *Production Specialist*

PAPERBACK ISBN: 978-1-4166-1868-3   ASCD product #114026

ASCD Member Book No. FY14-6A (April 2014 PSI+). ASCD Member Books mail to Premium (P),
Select (S), and Institutional Plus (I+) members on this schedule: Jan, PSI+; Feb, P; Apr, PSI+; May, P;
Jul, PSI+; Aug, P; Sep, PSI+; Nov, PSI+; Dec, P. For up-to-date details on membership, see www.ascd.org/
membership.

Also available as an e-book (see Books in Print for the ISBNs).

Quantity discounts: 10–49, 10%; 50+, 15%; 1,000+, special discounts (e-mail programteam@ascd.org
or call 800-933-2723, ext. 5773, or 703-575-5773). Also available in e-book formats. For desk copies,
go to www.ascd.org/deskcopy.

Library of Congress Cataloging-in-Publication Data

Rollins, Suzy Pepper.
    Learning in the fast lane : 8 ways to put ALL students on the road to academic success / Suzy Pepper
Rollins.
        pages cm
    Includes bibliographical references and index.
    ISBN 978-1-4166-1868-3 (paperback : alk. paper) 1. Remedial teaching. 2. Academic achievement.
I. Title.
    LB1029.R4R54 2014
    372.43—dc23
                                2013050764

23 22 21 20 19 18 17 16 15 14   1 2 3 4 5 6 7 8 9 10 11 12 13

LEARNING IN THE
FAST LANE

ASCD MEMBER BOOK

Many ASCD members received this book as a
member benefit upon its initial release.

Learn more at: **www.ascd.org/memberbooks**

For Doris Linder Chinnis

My mother, my mentor, my friend

LEARNING IN THE FAST LANE

8 WAYS TO PUT **ALL** STUDENTS ON THE ROAD TO ACADEMIC SUCCESS

Introduction

The best chance learners have to achieve success is the first time they go through a class or course. After that, the outlook becomes decidedly bleaker. When students fail to show mastery of concepts, and instruction turns to remediation, students' hopes dim and their academic options narrow.

My experience as a veteran classroom teacher, an educational consultant, and a coordinator of remedial programs in one of the largest school districts in the United States has led my thinking to one conclusion: to reach their potential, struggling students need the most powerful, effective instructional practices that research and practice have to offer. Tragically, the opposite often happens: instruction that aims to catch up lagging students or fix all their past problems ends up providing classroom experiences that are not compelling, rigorous, or engaging. Such instruction may inadvertently widen rather than close achievement gaps.

Accordingly, this book introduces a framework of eight high-impact instructional approaches that can move academically challenged students toward success. Rather than slowing students down, these instructional changes will enable students to grasp concepts more effectively and place them securely in the fast lane with their peers. These hands-on, ready-to-implement strategies will help you

- Use acceleration to immediately get students moving in the right direction.
- Make standards and learning goals explicit to students.

• Tackle many of the underlying causes of failure, such as lack of student motivation.

• Build students' self-efficacy so that they become active, academically hopeful participants in class.

• Encourage students to persevere rather than give up.

• Address the problem of skills gaps within the context of new learning.

• Improve students' vocabulary—one of the key deficits found in students who are at academic risk.

Students who are not making it academically have a great deal on the line. There is a well-established link between grade retention or course repetition and school dropout (Jimerson, Anderson, & Whipple, 2002). When students are compelled to repeat coursework, academic success and behavior can actually *decline* rather than improve.

Neither retention nor social promotion constitutes a viable academic plan for struggling students. Retention and remediation are costly to districts: teaching the same students the same subjects more than once piles up teacher allotments and administrative costs. Social promotion presents its own issues; moving students with known gaps forward to the next set of teachers doesn't fix anything.

The only solution is for students to legitimately master the concepts. The good news is, they can. Do they land in our classrooms with frustrating problems? Yes. They may not read at the desired level, have basic skills committed to memory, know the words they should, or even arrive with a pencil. But there is nothing more rewarding for teachers than to see the light of understanding dawn in a student's eyes, or watch a student who didn't think he could do it shoot up his hand with a correct answer.

The mission of this book is to provide help for those students who can be so challenging to teach yet have so much potential for academic growth. The eight overarching practices work together to address gaps in vocabulary, reading, basic skills, and student motivation in the context of new learning. Even better, these strategies foster academic achievement in *all* students—not just those who are at highest risk for academic failure. By bringing reflective, research-based, high-impact instruction to your classroom, you can help all your students get it the first time.

1

Acceleration:
Jump-Starting Students Who Are Behind

I recently came into a freshman remedial class to find students busily logging in to the school's basic-skills software. Those who were deemed the furthest behind, according to a diagnostic pre-test, practiced skills that were the furthest removed from the current curriculum. Students who weren't as far behind worked on skills from the previous year or two. Any connection between the skills the students practiced and the standards being introduced in their "regular" classes that same day was entirely coincidental. A young woman rolled her eyes at me as she entered her password on the keyboard: "We've been doing this program since 4th grade."

Hours away in a middle school classroom, bored students identified as requiring remedial interventions sat passively with their workbooks, practicing missing skills, while the higher-achieving students next door engaged collaboratively in hands-on, rigorous exploration aimed at a specific learning goal.

The traditional remedial approaches used in these and countless other classrooms focus on drilling isolated skills that bear little resemblance to current curriculum. Year after year, the same students are enrolled in remedial classes, and year after year, the academic gaps don't narrow. And no wonder: instead of addressing gaps in the context of new learning and helping students succeed in class *today*, remedial programs largely engage students in activities that connect to standards from years ago. Rather than build students' academic futures, remediation pounds away at the past. We spend significant amounts of time teaching in reverse, and then ask why students are not catching up to their peers.

This chapter provides thoughtful answers to a pressing question: *how can we help students with gaps from the past succeed today?* You will learn to provide a different, more effective type of support for struggling students that will yield immediate improvement in their academic progress, self-confidence, perseverance, and grades and test scores. In addition, you will see higher levels of participation and engagement and fewer incidences of off-task behavior.

Behind on the First Day of School

We know more about underperforming students today than ever before. Expansive color-coded spreadsheets detail every possible gap. Mountains of standardized test data reveal missed items from every subject area. Fractions, multiplication tables, parts of speech, order of operations, decimals, author's purpose, long division, branches of government, reading to infer . . . the list of things students should know (but don't) is daunting.

On the first day of school, many students are already behind. Marzano (2004) shares a gut-wrenching reality: what students already know when they enter the classroom—before we have even met them—is the strongest predictor of how well they will learn the new curriculum. Concepts, skills, and vocabulary from last semester, last year, and three grades ago can haunt students' efforts to acquire new information.

It works like this. As information is being taught, students' brains try to make sense of new concepts by linking and integrating the incoming barrage of information with prior knowledge. This *schema*, or individual storage unit of information, plays a critical role in new learning. Vacca and Vacca (2002) explain that when students' brains link background knowledge with new text, students are better at making inferences and retain information more effectively. Hirsch (2003) contends that prior knowledge about a topic speeds up learning by freeing up students' working memory so that they can connect to new information more readily. In short, students with background knowledge on a given topic are likely to grasp new information on that topic quickly and well

(Marzano, 2004). Conversely, a lack of adequate prior knowledge can create a misfire in the learning process.

For example, read the following short passage:

> Betsy had never tackled the Cement Mixer before. Although many fears cycled through her mind, her two main concerns were handling the backdoor and the lip. Her confidence rose, however, as she reminded herself that if she could just get into the barrel she had a good chance of winning, especially if conditions were cooking. She stared out at the horizon, shook her fist triumphantly in the air, and shouted, "I'm ready for you, Meat Grinder! I can handle the biggest Macker you can deliver!"

Now, in your own words, explain what Betsy is doing. Stumped? Every word is familiar and the reading level is basic, so what's the problem?

As it turns out, Betsy is a surfer. Terms like *backdoor, lip,* and even *Cement Mixer* have their own special meanings in the surfing lexicon. Without prior knowledge of Betsy's particular sport, true comprehension of this text is quite difficult. If you lack a schema for surfing, reading this passage would fail to spark a connection between prior knowledge and new information, and the text would be meaningless—and you'd fall behind in class.

The Trouble with Remediation

Just as a lack of background knowledge about surfing would lead to a lack of comprehension of the passage about Betsy, students who have insufficient academic background knowledge tend to have a multitude of missing academic pieces. Remediation, the correction of deficiencies, attempts to fix everything that has gone wrong in students' schooling—to fill in all those missing pieces. Unfortunately, many of those pieces may have nothing to do with what is happening today.

Remediation is based on the misconception that for students to learn new information, they must go back and master everything they missed. So, for example, all of the students who are weak in math—probably determined through a pre-test—are herded together and assigned a teacher who will reteach them basic math skills. The students who have the largest gaps and are thus the most academically vulnerable are sent the furthest distance back.

In the end, this remedial model may produce a student who can finally subtract two fractions; unfortunately, that student may now be a junior in high school. While the rest of her classmates moved forward, she moved backward. Reverse movement at a tedious pace with little relevance to today's standard will not catch students up to their peers. In fact, this model may contribute to widening gaps, as stronger students get even stronger while the weaker ones continue to sink further.

This failure to move forward can lead to decreased student motivation. Aside from the fact that students who have already grown to dislike math now have additional classes in the subject they despise, it's difficult to feel motivated when there's no apparent progress. In addition, remedial courses typically provide a surfeit of passive, basic-skills work and little real-world relevance. Boredom and futility creep in, and students often give up and shut down.

Why Acceleration Works

The primary focus of remediation is mastering concepts of the past. Acceleration, on the other hand, strategically prepares students for success in the present—*this* week, on *this* content. Rather than concentrating on a litany of items that students have failed to master, acceleration readies students for new learning. Past concepts and skills are addressed, but always in the purposeful context of future learning.

Acceleration jump-starts underperforming students into learning new concepts before their classmates even begin. Rather than being stuck in the remedial slow lane, students move ahead of everyone into the fast lane of learning. Acceleration provides a fresh academic start for students every week and creates opportunities for struggling students to learn alongside their more successful peers.

As we know, students learn faster and comprehend at a higher level when they have prior knowledge of a given concept. The correlation between academic background knowledge and achievement is staggering: prior knowledge can determine whether a 50th-percentile student sinks to the 25th percentile or rises to the 75th (Marzano, 2004). Accordingly, a crucial aspect of the acceleration model is putting key prior knowledge into place so that students have something to connect new information to. Rather than focus on everything students don't know about the concept, however, the core and acceleration teachers collaboratively and thoughtfully select the specific prior knowledge that will best help students grasp the upcoming standard.

Although the acceleration model does revisit basic skills, these skills are laser-selected, applied right away with the new content, and never taught in isolation. To prepare for a new concept or lesson, students in an acceleration program receive both instruction in prior knowledge and remediation of prerequisite skills that, if missing, may create barriers to the learning process. This strategic approach of preparing for the future while plugging a few critical holes from the past yields strong results.

Closely related to the prior knowledge piece of the acceleration model is vocabulary development. Gaps in prior knowledge are largely related to vocabulary (Marzano, 2004). For example, if you ask a student who has a rich understanding of fractions to write down everything she knows about the topic, she would likely list terms and concepts like *improper fraction, denominator, numerator, reciprocal, mixed number,* and *parts of a whole.* Likewise, a student asked to write down everything he knows about government would include terms like *bicameral, popular sovereignty, checks and balances, legislature,* and *federalism.* A sizable chunk of these students' prior knowledge consists of academic vocabulary. Therefore, a key step in the acceleration approach is to introduce new vocabulary (and review previously covered critical vocabulary that students may be missing) before the lesson begins in the core class.

Moving forward with students in an acceleration model requires teachers to carefully lay out the pieces of exactly what students need to know to learn the content at the desired pace. Before other students have even begun the unit, the accelerated group has gained an understanding of

- The real-world relevance and purpose of the concept.
- Critical vocabulary, including what the words look and sound like.
- The basic skills needed to master the concept.
- The new skills needed to master the concept.
- The big picture of where instruction is going.

Figure 1.1, which emerged from my work developing acceleration classes with teachers and leaders, presents a comparison of remediation and acceleration.

In my experience helping schools develop acceleration classes, the most common feedback I get from teachers is how quickly student confidence and participation increase. This marked improvement in students' self-efficacy makes perfect sense: concepts are placed directly in students' paths just in time for new learning in their core classrooms. Students' newfound knowledge increases the odds that they will know the correct responses to questions, and suddenly, raising their hands seems safer, and their fear of embarrassment diminishes.

As Sousa and Tomlinson (2011) explain, fear of peer reaction to an incorrect answer is a driving force in students' level of class participation. Conversely, positive feedback from teachers and peers ignites students'

FIGURE 1.1 Acceleration and Remediation: A Comparison		
	Acceleration	**Remediation**
Self-efficacy	• Self-confidence and engagement increase. • Academic progress is evident.	• Students perceive they're in the "slow class," and self-confidence and engagement decrease. • Backward movement leads to a sense of futility and lack of progress.
Basic skills	• Skills are hand-picked just in time for new concepts. • Students apply skills immediately.	• Instruction attempts to reteach every missing skill. • Skills are taught in isolation and not applied to current learning.
Prior knowledge	• Key prior knowledge is provided ahead of time, enabling students to connect to new information.	• Typically does not introduce prior knowledge that connects to new learning.
Relevance	• Treats relevance as critical component to student motivation and memory.	• Relevance is not seen as a priority.
Connection to core class	• Instruction is connected to core class; ongoing collaboration is emphasized.	• Instruction is typically isolated from core class.
Pacing and direction	• Active, fast-paced, hands-on. • Forward movement; goal is for students to learn on time with peers.	• Passive, with focus on worksheets or basic software programs. • Backward movement; goal is for students to "catch up" to peers.

desire to keep succeeding. Spikes in self-efficacy, Pajares (2006) found, can lead students to engage more, work harder, stick it out longer, and achieve at higher levels. Students are able to perceive genuine progress, so this increase in self-efficacy is not superficial; it is the brain's response to real success. Acceleration can fuel new hope and motivation in students who once perceived their academic situation as hopeless.

Implementing Acceleration

There are a few logistics to address when implementing an acceleration program. The first step is identifying students who would be good candidates for acceleration, typically by reviewing standardized test data. Some schools focus just on "bubble" students—those who are right on the verge of passing their standardized tests. However, some schools in which I have consulted, after realizing acceleration's potential to yield significant results, expand their acceleration classes to include students with more significant gaps.

Another issue to address is deciding who teaches the acceleration classes. The teachers of acceleration classes may be either students' regular content-area teachers or separate teachers. There are pragmatic reasons to schedule students with their core teachers as much as possible. For example, when students attend acceleration classes with their core teachers, teachers can make just the right instructional moves during acceleration to facilitate student success in the later core class. When a different teacher is used for acceleration, daily communication and coordination of curriculum pacing become essential to maximize the program's effectiveness. The acceleration teacher *must* know where the core teacher's instruction is to be able to prepare students for success.

Carving out time is another important issue to address when beginning an acceleration program. Some schools schedule a short time (usually around 45 minutes) at the beginning of each day in which all students receive acceleration or enrichment. I've known schools to refer to this time as anything from ELT (Extended Learning Time) to Ram Time (schools can replace *Ram* with their own mascot) to Fast Lane Class (my favorite).

A second option is to incorporate acceleration into electives, specials, or pullouts. This model often provides more time than the ELT model and is typically used for the "double dose" approach, in which students receive extra instruction in problem subjects. Elementary and middle schools often use an additional teacher for this time, which enables core teachers to use this period for planning. The person in this acceleration role varies by school but is often a special educator or remedial teacher. In high schools, the core teachers often teach their own acceleration classes.

Before- and after-school tutoring or Saturday school is a third option. My first experience with acceleration was through tutoring at the middle school level. I phoned parents and explained to them that this was not going to be traditional tutoring—that our mission was to get their children ahead of the game. Parents were more than willing to make a commitment to ensure their children's attendance. Every day, for 30 minutes before school and 30 minutes after school, I accelerated the group in their trouble courses of math and science. Within a week, core teachers reported significant gains in student participation (one of the key components of success) and achievement. A thrilled science teacher said of one student, "He hasn't made over a 50 on a test all year, and he passed this one with flying colors!"

Students in an acceleration class should always be a session or two ahead of their peers in the core class. On a block schedule, one class period (typically around 90 minutes long) is generally sufficient. If the school is implementing acceleration through shorter tutoring sessions, two sessions are workable for jump-starting the content. These times are just general guidelines; however much time schools are able to set aside can be maximized with acceleration. The duration and frequency of acceleration classes vary according to individual schools' schedules as well as students' progress, which can be assessed through ongoing observation.

The Acceleration Framework

Accelerating students is not pre-teaching; that risks tedium. Rather, it is an enriching experience designed to stimulate thinking, develop concrete models, introduce vocabulary, scaffold critical missing pieces, and introduce new concepts just prior to acquisition of new learning. Students are provided with just enough prior knowledge to latch on more readily to new concepts. There is a symbiotic, complementary relation-ship between "the core" and "the more"—that is, the core content and the supplemental learning and support provided by acceleration. The core and the more share the single purpose of helping students master standards the first time.

The acceleration model includes several crucial components, which I have developed as six steps over time, first through my work with my own students and later through my work with numerous schools tweaking the acceleration model. Each step is essential to student learning and motivation.

Step 1: Generate Thinking, Purpose, Relevance, and Curiosity

One or two days before the core class begins the concept or standard, acceleration begins with a thought-provoking, hands-on activity that encompasses the big idea of the standard. Typically working in small groups or pairs, students explore the new concept by generating their own formulas, developing ideas, discovering patterns, discussing observations, or examining the content's real-world relevance. In math or science, the teacher can use some of this time to develop concrete representations before embarking on abstract ideas. In all content areas, this step speaks to students' need to answer the question "What does this have to do with me?"

Success starters, which vary by standard and content area, are a good way to get students to plunge into the new content and gain curiosity and confidence. Here are some examples (see Chapter 3 for a more in-depth discussion of success starters).

In math, students could

• Use string to measure the circumference of a jar lid, then discuss the relationship of the circumference and the diameter using the string as a guide.
  • Go on a scavenger hunt for items with surface area.
  • Sort angles by similarities or differences.
  • Read a picture book about fractions.
  • Spin a game spinner and then discuss why the game may not be fair and determine what would make it fair.

In science, students could

- Draw items from bags, determine which ones they believe are renewable and which ones are nonrenewable, and explain their reasoning.
- Choose a pretend animal from a grab bag and brainstorm how their animal may adapt physically and behaviorally to changing environmental conditions, such as a drought or flooding.
- Respond in writing to pictures of earthquake damage.
- Watch the weather report and jot down vocabulary used.
- Tour the school as environmentalists searching for evidence of the building's carbon footprint.

In social studies, students could

- Develop their own Bill of Rights.
- Create a rapid-fire list of everything they know about government at any level.
- Examine websites of local banks and list common characteristics.
- Respond to a slideshow of images from World War I using just adjectives.

In language arts, students could

- Watch a short clip of a cartoon that uses alliteration and jot down examples.
- Identify elements of a story in a piece of literature similar to one that will be studied in class.
- Piece together a sort of the parts of an essay.
- Create a sort on tricky verb conjugations.

Why step 1 should never be skipped: Students who struggle academically are more likely to shut down on concepts that they perceive as irrelevant. Their motivation to work increases in direct correlation with their perception of the content's value and interest level. Right out of the gate, success starters create value, relevance, and interest and foster both motivation and long-term retention of content.

Step 2: Clearly Articulate the Learning Goal and Expectations

The placement of this step is quite purposeful. Step 1 showed students the real-world relevance of the new concept and triggered their curiosity. By step 2, their brains should be primed for the teacher's introduction of the learning goal—for example, "What we just explored is actually the first part of the standard we'll be learning" or "In 40 minutes, you will be able to compare and contrast the core, the mantle, and the crust."

Explicit learning expectations are essential, but students often lack clarity about what they are studying. Learning goals are the basis of student learning, and this step is too important to rely on a wordy posted standard. Leahy, Lyon, Thompson, and Wiliam (2005) concur that simply posting a standard is rarely successful because standards tend not to be written in student-friendly language. Stiggins (2007) holds that standards should be deconstructed into classroom targets that unfold into opportunities for daily formative assessment. Personally, I advocate for standards walls (discussed further in Chapter 2), which provide a visual avenue for articulating the patterns of standards. Standards walls help clarify for students the progression of learning—how separate goals crescendo into an understanding of the big picture of a concept. Providing these patterns for learning has an additional benefit: Willis (2006) explains that delivering new information to students in a way that builds connections to other learning enhances brain cell activity, leading to improved long-term memory and retrieval.

Why step 2 should never be skipped: All students, but particularly those at risk of failure, benefit from explicitly stated, student-friendly learning goals. Vague references to academic expectations have little value. Without specific goals, students can lose sight of the purpose of learning, and class becomes a blur of papers and exercises to complete rather than a logical progression of learning that leads to an important goal.

Step 3: Scaffold and Practice Essential Prerequisite Skills

(*Note: steps 3 and 4 can be switched in sequence or taught in tandem.*)

After step 2, acceleration pauses as students briefly move backward to remediate the deficits that would present a barrier to learning the new standard. To edit a potentially long list of gaps, complete the following statement:

Students could master the new standard if they just knew

_____.

Next, start filling in the high-priority gaps you identified. For example, if knowledge of integer rules is essential, have students create bookmarks listing integer rules and then provide guided practice reviewing integers. If students need to be able to multiply decimals, shore up their skills and develop a scaffolding device, such as a cheat sheet with an example. You can create these scaffolding cheat sheets with examples of anything students need reinforcement in, such as parts of speech or types of sentences (simple, compound, and complex). If a separate teacher is providing acceleration, the regular teacher should communicate these essential prerequisite skills so that students can shore up these areas before the lesson.

Figure 1.2 demonstrates judicious use of scaffolding: if students do not remember all of their multiplication facts, you can create a chart that includes just the ones they do not know. As students learn facts, take them off the chart. The purpose of scaffolding devices is to enable

FIGURE 1.2 Scaffolding Example: Partial Multiplication Table			
	6	**7**	**8**
6	36	42	48
7	42	49	56
8	48	56	64

students to access the rigor of the standard. Without them, students can get mired in their gaps, and frustration sets in. It's just as important not to provide too much scaffolding, however; keep tabs on each student's progress to get an idea of when you need to reduce or withdraw support.

Why step 3 should never be skipped: Without this step, students may embark on their work with enthusiasm but use the incorrect integer signs on every answer, or the decimal may somehow fall in the wrong place. All that work and no payoff! Scaffolding prerequisite skills in context allows students to realize success on new content.

Step 4: Introduce New Vocabulary and Review Prior Vocabulary

Because vocabulary understanding is developed over the course of time and is a key component of prior knowledge, acceleration students in particular benefit from rich vocabulary experiences. An effective starting point is to create a *TIP:* a continually growing anchor wall chart that includes vocabulary *terms, information* on those terms, and *pictures* of the terms. As words are introduced, they are added to the TIP. The TIP provides a constant reference point for students, so when a student is asked, for example, "What part of a cell is most like the water boy on a football team?" she can glance over at the TIP for guidance. Figure 1.3 shows an example of the TIP process for an acceleration math class. Once the term *circumference* has been introduced and defined, the class would come up with the picture together, with the teacher suggesting, "Circumference is

FIGURE 1.3 TIP Chart: Math Vocabulary		
Term	**Information**	**Picture**
Circumference	Distance around a circle	circumference
Diameter	Straight line passing through the center of a circle	diameter

the distance around a circle, so how about we draw a circle with arrows showing circumference?"

The TIP is a good start, but multiple representations are crucial to build students' deep, sustained knowledge of vocabulary. Jenkins, Stein, and Wysocki (1984) contend that students' sixth exposure to a word is around when they begin to truly internalize and be able to use it. Acceleration gives students a head start on this process.

A key to vocabulary retention is immersing students in hands-on, playful, multisensory vocabulary experiences. During acceleration classes, vocabulary development practices should be memorable, hands-on, and interactive. In Chapter 5, I discuss powerful vocabulary strategies to use in acceleration instruction.

Why step 4 should never be skipped: Providing targeted students with advance knowledge of new vocabulary reaps major benefits in the core class. As the heterogeneous group begins the new unit, acceleration students realize success and gain confidence: "Oh, I know what that word means!"

Step 5: Dip into the New Concept

During the first four steps, students have already begun work on the new concept. They have established the concept's relevance and purpose and have a clear idea of the learning goals. They are shoring up their gaps in prerequisite skills in the context of new learning, and vocabulary development is under way. Now students are poised for going a bit deeper into the new content. This is the part they really appreciate: they get to do some things that their classmates have not even seen yet!

In math, this "dipping in" may amount to some guided practice on whiteboards (used individually or in pairs) calculating perimeter, or a scavenger hunt to locate different angles. In language arts, students may score sample papers using a writing rubric. The science acceleration class might examine pictures of the circulatory system. These activities will not be duplicated in the core class; the repetition would lead to boredom. Instead, the acceleration time sets students up for mastering standards in the core class, so that when a new concept is introduced, students can say, "I know something about that!"

Why step 5 should never be skipped: Students' self-efficacy and enthusiasm soar as they are, possibly for the first time in their lives, ahead of the class.

Step 6: Conduct Formative Assessment Frequently

Because the goal of acceleration is to help students learn content in their core class the first time, it is essential to collect ongoing data of student progress. There should be a continual flow of formative assessment information between the core teachers and the "more" teachers, although the same teacher may serve both roles.

Acceleration lends itself beautifully to ongoing, transparent formative assessment that yields timely, detailed feedback from teachers and peers. Having students hold up their answers on individual whiteboards fits perfectly, as do strategies like sorts and problem solving on sticky notes. Or students can work on chart paper on the floor or at their desks. Essentially, anything that will help teachers continually "see" what students know provides valuable information on where students are and where they need to go. Formative assessment strategies are further explored in Chapter 4.

Why step 6 should never be skipped: Instructional adjustments in acceleration are immediate and ongoing based on student data. This is not a class in which papers are scored traditionally and returned days later. Students targeted for acceleration have an urgent need for real success right now. For that to occur, teachers must use primarily "soft" formative assessment to provide descriptive feedback.

Reflections on Acceleration

In my experience with the acceleration model, I have found that teachers and students alike can feel a strong gravitational pull to revert to remediation. Students may lack confidence in completing homework on their own or need tutoring on current work from the core class. Such bumps in the road can shift the focus from moving students forward to helping them survive today. Teachers report that when a test is looming, students feel an urgent need for help with preparation and have difficulty focusing on learning concepts beyond the test. In cases when students' need for review or remediation is especially pressing, my advice is to split the time in two: first help students review, and then introduce the next concept.

Accelerating students as a method of boosting academic achievement is as much a shift in mind-set as it is in instruction. It will always be difficult to resist the urge to try to fill in students' gaps and fix, fix, fix everything that went wrong in the past. And it is all too easy to slip back into remedial worksheets when students have so many missing pieces. But don't give in to the temptation. Adherence to the acceleration instructional model is crucial. The model is carefully designed and highly tactical: your goal is to shore up just what students need to be successful on new concepts.

The following section highlights a school whose teachers decided to make the change from remediation to acceleration. The results they observed in their students mirror what I have seen and heard in many schools.

In the fall of 2012, the math teachers at East Jackson High School were ready to try something new. Dissatisfied with test scores from the previous spring, they embarked on a different path to help students who were struggling to master the content.

The biggest change came from Julie Bruce, who taught the support class, or double dose. In the past, she had always provided remediation, typically spending class time helping students with homework and revisiting concepts they had missed in the past. Not this year. She announced to her students, "I'm not worried about what you've already learned; I'm worried about what you're going to learn."

Instead of retreading old ground, Julie began getting her students ready for their upcoming core class. She introduced the new concepts and explained the vocabulary words as they came up, in student-friendly terms. Students became accustomed to hearing, "This is what you're going to see tomorrow." She routinely stayed a day or two ahead of the core teachers.

At first, students were a bit wary of the new approach. But soon enough, Julie began seeing positive changes: one student announced, "This is the first day in math class that I wasn't confused!" while another proclaimed, "This is the first time ever in my school career that I could answer questions in math class."

Sandy Akin, one of the core teachers, noticed a change in the confidence level of the acceleration students in her heterogeneous class: they had begun participating more and asking questions. Sandy commented, "These aren't students who misbehaved. If they were lost, they didn't say anything; they just shut down." She attributed their increase in self-efficacy to the jump-start they received in their support class: "After starting acceleration, they came in the room with more confidence."

East Jackson teachers credit ongoing collaboration as a critical component of acceleration in their school. Core teachers quickly discovered that if Julie taught a concept a bit differently in acceleration, it threw students: "That's not how Ms. Bruce showed us!" Accordingly, teachers learned to get on the same page in terms of curriculum pacing, instructional approach to new concepts, and assessment.

Their reflective, collaborative approach to acceleration paid off: 72 percent of the support students passed the state end-of-course math test, compared with 50 percent the prior year. Among students with disabilities, 80 percent passed, compared with 20 percent the prior year. The acceleration students' test scores improved overall by 6 percent.

Julie's concluding thoughts on her school's move toward acceleration? "I'm a believer."

Checklist for acceleration:

❑ Students can clearly articulate the meaning of today's learning goal.

❑ Students receive scaffolding for prerequisite skills in the context of new learning.

❑ Vocabulary development is hands-on and ongoing and focuses on clearly identified academic vocabulary terms.

❑ Remediation provided is just in time and set in the context of new learning.

❑ Assessment is visible and yields immediate feedback.

❑ Students largely work cooperatively in a safe learning environment.

❑ Students are learning the big idea of new concepts in advance of their core-class peers.

❑ The acceleration teacher and the core-class teacher engage in ongoing collaboration regarding pacing and student progress.

2

Standards Walls: Transforming Standards into Clear Learning Goals

The first-period bell sounds in a high school social studies class. Students scrawl notes on key U.S. industrialists during a lecture laden with vocabulary words like *tariff, laissez-faire, patent, Bessemer process, cartel, monopoly, oligopoly, social Darwinism, robber barons,* and *vertical* and *horizontal integration.*

The bell rings, and students shuffle down the hall to science. Today's class focuses on the structure and composition of atoms, and terms such as *nucleus, electrons, protons, neutrons, quarks, atomic numbers, elements,* and *isotopes* fly around the room. The homework assignment is to memorize a list of symbols of common chemical elements.

Third period begins, and the teacher passes out a test on probability. In addition to proficiency in the math problems, learners need a deep understanding of the terms *conditional, dependent, independent, mutually exclusive,* and *expected value.*

After a short lunch break, students proceed to language arts. About halfway through reading *To Kill a Mockingbird,* the class is discussing key concepts like *mood, point of view, foreshadowing,* and *irony.* Students are asked to compare the character Atticus Finch with a current-day public figure.

Last period brings health class, in which students explore the fascinating world of *fallopian tubes* and *ovaries*.

The final bell sounds, and students head home. "What did you learn in school today?" parents ask. "I honestly couldn't tell you. Something about Atticus Finch being a robber baron? No, wait—I think there's a monopoly on ovaries. . . ." The following are all-too-typical examples of questions and answers exchanged during classroom observations:

- *What are you doing in math?* "A sheet."
- *What are you learning in science today?* "We're doing a lab."
- *What are you studying in social studies?* "We're taking notes and watching a video."

A mind-numbing barrage of information and vocabulary swirl around students all day long. How do they keep it all straight? Many don't. Students often have vague ideas of what they are learning but lack explicit understanding of the standards being taught. Rather than understanding how standards build on one another to create a big picture of important concepts, they often perceive school as a series of disparate assignments to complete.

The Trouble with Posting Standards

For students to master content the first time they learn it, they must first possess a clear understanding of what they are learning and how the concepts connect. What does today's learning have to do with yesterday's, or tomorrow's? What about the stuff covered last month?

The traditional approach to communicating standards is to post them somewhere in the classroom. This practice is woefully inadequate for articulating the bar that students must meet. Dense text mounted on a wall (usually in a font size that is barely discernible) diminishes the standards and places them on par with the lunchroom menu. Students' academic lives depend on their mastery of the standards, which requires a clear comprehension of the standards' meaning and rigor. Simply posting them does not support students in understanding the standards' purpose, the expectations they set, or the connections among them.

Why Standards Walls Work

Standards walls answer the question "What are we learning?" in a clear, concise format. They include everything students need in one place, including learning objectives, vocabulary, and work samples. While retaining the standards' rigor and purity, they jettison the usual murky litany of items and instead present the standards and learning goals in a logical, readable sequence that students understand, displaying a clear progression of content and explicit patterns of learning. In addition, they are written in student-friendly language. The words used in standards should never be a mystery to students. Indeed, explicit expectations are where first-time mastery begins.

Students and teachers in classrooms with standards walls are able to articulate the lesson's learning objective quickly and accurately. The walls are like a directory at a gigantic shopping mall saying, "You are here!" Read on to learn how to implement this powerful tool.

Implementing Standards Walls

Before students embark on the journey laid out by standards, teachers must make decisions about the path students will take. The best way to construct standards walls is through teacher collaboration. The process fosters professional conversations that bring valuable clarity and direction to the curriculum.

Keep in mind that it's important to strike a balance between making standards understandable to students and maintaining the purity and intended rigor of standards. For example, it's best not to change the verbs of standards and learning goals but instead to insert synonyms adjacent to them to bridge vocabulary understandings. The following steps form a useful guide for teachers as they create their own standards walls:

1. Begin by creating a concept map (see page 25 for more on this). Identify the overarching enduring understanding or essential question of the unit. Write this in the center of a large piece of chart paper. (Note: this should not simply be a unit topic, such as "World War I," but a thought-provoking question or concept, such as "What factors led to World War I?")

2. Identify the learning goals from the standard that would move students toward deep comprehension of the long-term goal in the center. Construct verb/noun learning goals (more on these on page 25), and place those in sequence around the central enduring understanding. With particularly lengthy standards, it may be useful to present a few learning goals at a time, adding to them as learning progresses. Once students have become accustomed to standards walls, however, they may derive more benefit from seeing the entire learning picture at once.

3. Place a sticky arrow or other symbol at the starting point—that is, the initial learning goal that the unit will address.

4. Collaboratively create a list of essential academic vocabulary words related to the standard. The purpose of this step is to come up with a vocabulary plan for the unit, recognizing that students need multiple, varied exposures to truly master new words. During this step, also design the framework for classroom TIP charts. Words should be introduced one by one, as students first encounter them, or as part of a preview of reading—not all at once.

5. Either before or after the lesson opener, identify for students the lesson's learning goal on the standards wall; the arrow should be pointing at this goal. If you like, you can assign students to place the arrow in the correct spot. As students complete assignments, post their work adjacent to the relevant learning goal. In addition, refer to the wall frequently during the lesson and, particularly, during the final quick check for the learning episode.

The following section explains in depth the components that are integral to these steps.

Components of Standards Walls

Through research, trial and error, and observation of hundreds of teachers and students in action, I have identified three components of standards walls that I believe most effectively support student learning: the concept map, the TIP chart, and student work.

Component 1: Concept Map

Transforming a posted standard from a passive, obscure check-off item into a highly effective instructional tool begins with the creation of a concept map. The concept map is in essence an illustrated advance organizer. Marzano, Pickering, and Pollock (2001), in a distillation of research on the effects of advance organizers, reported a 20 percent gain in student achievement resulting from the use of these tools.

The concept map is created on chart paper, prominently displayed and large enough to be seen by students in every corner of the room. It is a permanent fixture throughout the unit. The teacher (or student) moves a sticky arrow or other symbol around the map as the class progresses through the standard. Each strand that emanates from the center is a learning goal, which equates to a daily essential question. As students master each learning goal, they move closer to being able to expound on the unit's central enduring understanding. This map includes two important parts:

1. The unit's overarching enduring understanding or essential question. This concept rests in the center of the map. As learners progress through each connected learning goal, they deepen their understanding of this big concept.

2. Explicit learning goals that remain true to the rigor of the standard yet are understandable to students. These learning goals retain the main verbs and nouns of the connecting standard but are rephrased in student-friendly language and arranged on the concept map in a more intuitive, visual manner.

   a. *Verbs:* The verbs are the action of the learning goal. *Comparing and contrasting* is a different skill than *explaining,* just as *evaluating* an argument looks different from *identifying* one. Students may have difficulty grasping the meaning of these verbs and differentiating them from one another, so it can be helpful to add a parenthetical explanation in student-friendly terms on the map. For example, next to *determine,* you might insert the text "*(make conclusions about).*"

   b. *Nouns:* The nouns refer to the content that students will learn. These are the heart of the concepts—the informational part. For example, students will *use* (verb) Greek and Latin *roots* (nouns). In science, students will *explain* (verb) the *impact* of *water* on *life* (nouns).

Let's look at how we might transform a confusing, verbose high school U.S. government standard into a clear concept map. The format below is what students typically see posted as their course of study. What should be a simple answer to the question "What are you learning in government today?" becomes obfuscated:

> The student will demonstrate knowledge of the federal system of government described in the United States Constitution.
>   a. Explain the relationship of state governments to the national government.
>   b. Define the difference between enumerated and implied powers.
>   c. Describe the extent to which power is shared.
>   d. Identify powers denied to state and national governments.
>   e. Analyze the ongoing debate that focuses on the balance of power between state and national governments. (Georgia Department of Education, 2012)

Is it any wonder students are not quite sure what they are learning? Now look at this same standard, reconceived as a concept map (see Figure 2.1).

This format is much easier for students to grasp than a solid block of text is. The overarching essential question is clearly phrased and easily understood, and every student, no matter what the level of his or her individual mastery of the standard is, can find the arrow and see that today's learning goal is to "define the difference between enumerated and implied powers." In addition, students can see that beneath this goal's two new vocabulary words—*enumerated* and *implied*—are two helpful synonyms.

Most important, this map enables students to see the progress they are making. We can surmise that the class has already "explained the relationship between state and national governments." Teachers frequently tell me how exciting it is to move the arrow to the next learning goal; they often assign students this honor.

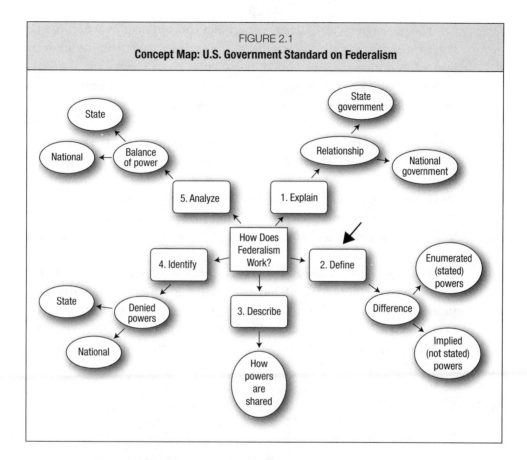

FIGURE 2.1
Concept Map: U.S. Government Standard on Federalism

Each learning goal may be expressed as an essential question or an "I can" statement on the board—for example, "What is the difference between enumerated and implied powers?" (essential question) or "I can explain the difference between enumerated and implied powers" ("I can" statement). As students master each branch of the concept map, they move closer to the ultimate goal of the standard. In this case, students will have a deep understanding of how federalism works. At this point, the patterns of the standard become clear, and students realize how learning goals interlace and build on one another to become a larger concept.

The image in Figure 2.2 shows part of a concept map in action in Ms. Patel's 8th grade classroom. Instead of trying to decipher (or just ignoring) a lengthy, small-print standard, students can easily see that today's learning goal is to explain equal slopes. As students demonstrate mastery, their work samples will be posted next to the learning goal.

Figure 2.3 shows part of a concept map in a middle school class that is in its second year of using standards walls. The teacher, Mr. Farnsworth, has witnessed significant growth in students' ability to articulate learning objectives. When I visited the classroom, I asked one student, "What are you learning today in math?" Without pausing, he responded, "Here, let me *show* you what we are doing." He reached over and pointed to the day's learning goal and explained, "We are graphing solutions on a number line."

How much to display at a time on a concept map is a decision that calls for careful thought. With lengthier standards, there is merit to initially placing just a few connected learning goals on the wall and adding on to them as students progress. Other teachers report benefits to putting it all out there at once, particularly once students become accustomed

FIGURE 2.2
Concept Map: Math Standard on Slope

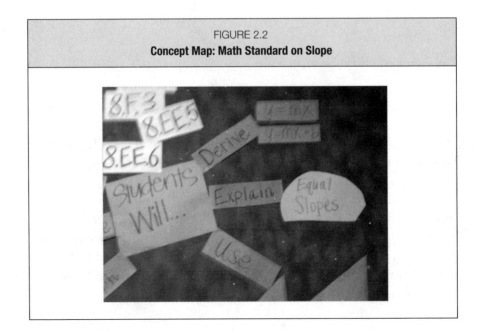

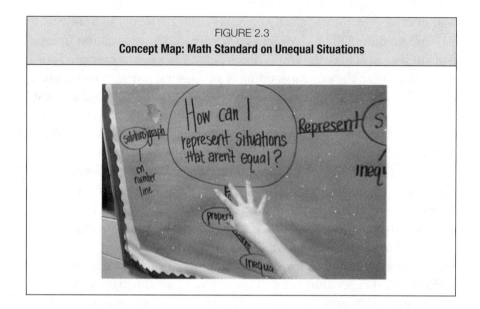

FIGURE 2.3
Concept Map: Math Standard on Unequal Situations

to standards walls. Whichever approach you prefer, keep in mind the ultimate goal of concept maps: they are instructional tools designed to help students access the curriculum every day, not wall decorations to be posted and ignored.

Component 2: TIP Chart

The sheer volume of content-area vocabulary students face is daunting. During middle school, for example, the typical student will encounter almost 1,000 new words in science, math, social studies, and language arts (Marzano, 2004). Complicating the instructional challenge of teaching this huge quantity of words is the fact that to gain meaningful, long-term understanding, students require multiple, varied exposures to new terms and must use new vocabulary in different ways repeatedly over time.

As we know, inadequate academic vocabulary often presents a barrier to new learning. The use of a TIP (which some acceleration students will already be using) helps remove that obstacle. Recall that the TIP is a continually growing anchor wall chart that includes vocabulary *terms, information* on those terms, and *pictures* of the terms. Placed on the standards wall in close proximity to the concept map, the TIP works according to our understanding of how vocabulary is learned. The expectation is not that students will have the words down pat after their first exposure, but rather that vocabulary understanding is an ongoing process that builds on itself. The class adds each new word to the TIP with great fanfare, first writing the word on the wall, then collaborating to arrive at a concise definition, and, finally, creating a memorable visual depiction of the term. This TIP process helps implant the new word in students' memories.

The TIP also provides an opportunity for teachers to pronounce new words for students. According to Tankersley (2005), all students benefit from hearing new vocabulary words spoken correctly before they are asked to use the words on their own. The word *façade,* for example, sounds a lot different than it looks. Students with vocabulary gaps particularly benefit from explicit, frequent discussions using these words. In addition, Tankersley affirms the effectiveness of organizing words into picture maps that provide visuals and memory cues for students. In the sample TIP in Figure 2.4, difficult words are combined with student-friendly explanations and picture references, such as an image of *seashells by the seashore* for the word *alliteration.*

With the TIP in place as an easily accessible reference, students are better able to answer questions in class. When the teacher asks, "Is 'Love Is a Battlefield' an example of a metaphor or a simile?" students can glance over at the TIP to refresh their memory and confidently announce, "Metaphor." Conversations in social studies not only sound a lot different but also include more student voices. When the teacher asks, "What's the difference between enumerated and implied powers?" every student is able to respond, "Enumerated powers are clearly stated and implied ones are not."

Vocabulary can overwhelm students, but the ongoing use of this simple device provides continual support and access to words as students are learning them. In a high school AP math class I observed recently, the teacher used the TIP strategy for the first time, with students using personal TIPs at their desks in addition to the wall TIP. Over the course of a two-day lesson, probably a dozen discipline-specific words were introduced. In addition to the TIP, the teacher used collaborative strategies to

| FIGURE 2.4 |||
| **ELA TIP Chart** |||
T	**I**	**P**
Personification	Objects take on traits of people	 (Slumbering moon)
Onomatopoeia	Imitates sound it describes	 (The word *howl* mimics what a howl actually sounds like.)
Alliteration	Repetition of first sound	 (She sells seashells by the seashore.)

make the lesson highly engaging. At the end of the lesson, I asked students which part of the lesson they believed was most effective for them. I was expecting them to say that their favorite part was working with friends, but over and over students responded, "The TIP." One student said, "The assignment would have been very difficult without the TIP." If students at the highest academic tier felt the power of a TIP, imagine how much it could help students who are barely hanging on.

Together, the concept map and the TIP organize learning for students' brains; clustering critical information into a neat, understandable diagram takes the mess out of standards. These visual representations of essential learning goals and vocabulary are so impactful that when standards walls come down for a unit test, students often continue to glance over at the bare walls, where they can still "see" the information they need.

Component 3: Student Work

Student work samples make up the third portion of standards walls. Rather than (or in addition to) posting work in hallways or on bulletin boards, student work samples are posted right on the wall, in context. In addition to recognizing student work, this practice underlines the meaning and explicit expectations of the standards and enables all students to see what quality work for a given learning goal or standard strand looks like. While the standard as a whole can seem unmanageable, when it's broken into parts, students can better achieve proximal goals. Posting student work shows how each learning objective contributes to the big picture of the enduring understanding in the center of the concept map.

The standards wall in Ms. Jackson's middle school language arts class, part of which is pictured in Figure 2.5, shows a clear learning goal

FIGURE 2.5
Language Arts Standards Wall with Student Work

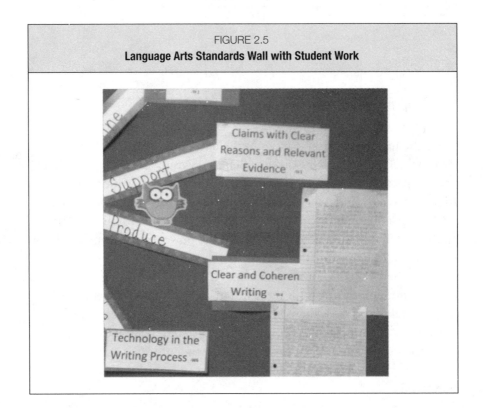

(denoted by the owl rather than an arrow): students will "produce clear and coherent writing." Adjacent to the learning goal are student examples of clear and coherent writing. Language arts standards present a unique opportunity for articulating learning goals, since classes continually incorporate reading, grammar, and writing throughout the year. Whereas in other content areas, a unit is more of a separate entity with clear boundaries, in language arts, students may have three learning goals across these arenas. For that reason, I encourage teacher collaboration in planning construction of language arts standards walls, which remain affixed throughout the year.

Reflections on Standards Walls

Initially, creating standards walls may seem a bit odd. It's something new and different. I had the honor of observing a teacher on her first day of using a standards wall. She had already begun the unit and was a bit nervous about how students would react to this new addition to their class. As students came in, their heads immediately turned toward the chart paper filled with colorful diagramming. The teacher laughed and asked, "Notice something different today?" Then she pointed on the concept map to a recently covered learning goal and asked, "What did we learn Monday?" Students called out, "We used and applied surface area of spheres." She responded, "Right. Now, what do you think we're going to learn today?" Every student understood that the class was going to learn about using and applying the volume of spheres. Right away, they were able to intuit the structure and meaning of the concept map.

Standards can be overwhelming to students: the large volume of text coupled with unfamiliar words can inhibit their understanding of a concept's big picture. The brain seeks patterns to make sense of things, and standards walls help with that process, providing a systematic approach to standards' language and progression and giving students what they need to grasp new content the first time. There are already so many academic hurdles for these students; knowing what they are learning today should not be one of them.

Checklist for standards walls:

- ❏ The unit's overarching essential question or enduring understanding is clear.
- ❏ The wall clearly depicts today's learning goal.
- ❏ The learning goal is clearly articulated by the teacher and students throughout class, specifically during the opening and closing minutes.
- ❏ The TIP includes academic vocabulary, definitions in student-friendly terms, and pictures or examples.
- ❏ The wall displays student work that demonstrates mastery of learning goals.
- ❏ Every student can clearly read the words on the standards wall.

3

Success Starters:
Sparking Student Success Right Away

The opening minutes of class are often the most hectic. One student digs for a signed test to return and dumps his entire backpack on the floor in a frantic search. Another student has a withdrawal form that needs to be completed right now because her dad's car is idling in a no-parking zone. Two other students swear that they will die of dehydration if they cannot get water right this second. Attendance needs to be taken and entered into the computer in the next two minutes. The office is calling to report a bus change, and please don't forget to have a student deliver the food-drive collection box to room 214 by the end of the day. Oh, and the assistant principal is at the door and needs a quick word. . . .

Thank goodness, there's a warm-up for students on the board, so the teacher can handle all these administrative tasks! Right? Well, not quite.

The Trouble with Warm-Ups

Warm-ups, or bell ringers, do have some merit. Often review-oriented, they are designed to get students into their seats and quickly on task. In language arts, students' task is often to locate grammatical errors in text excerpts. In math, students get a few review problems to solve. Social studies and science teachers may begin by writing a handful of review questions on the board.

Although warm-ups may have some academic benefit, they are largely designed as self-regulatory work to keep students busy while the teacher takes care of the managerial side of education. They are a classroom management technique: students quickly learn the routine and readily fall into the habit. They are useful, operationally, to the school building.

The trouble with warm-ups is that they are quite possibly the opposite of what students' brains need during the opening minutes of class. Bell ringers often represent missed opportunities to provide what would stimulate the brain: relevance, novelty, interest, and a connection to prior knowledge. Usually by the time a warm-up has concluded, enthusiasm has waned, intellectual curiosity is flatlining, and the big idea for today—the magnificently important learning goal—is buried deep inside lesson time.

Worse, what often follows the warm-up is homework review. For some students, the homework was simple, whereas others may have a few concerns that need to be addressed. Still other students didn't do it, can't find it, or don't even recall it being assigned. Top students must now endure a replay of the homework they already understood while lower-achieving students squirm or pretend to search for their papers. (Students in the middle of the pack may reap some benefit.)

Consider warm-ups and homework review from the perspective of a student hanging from the tiniest of academic threads. This student has likely experienced difficulty with the homework and may have given up on it or feel too embarrassed to let anyone see it. Now he's feeling anxious about being called on about last night's work. The warm-up itself may offer a modicum of success, if it covers content the student has retained, but then again, maybe it doesn't. Right out of the gate, class is going badly for this student, and the downward spiral continues from there.

The Power of the Opening Minutes

The opening minutes of a lesson hold tremendous potential for all learners; in fact, Sousa (2008) explains that students are most apt to remember what is taught at the beginning of a lesson; the second-highest peak comes during the last part of class. This phenomenon is referred to as the *primacy-recency effect*, meaning students best retain what was taught first and what was taught most recently.

Scheduling administrative tasks, bell ringers, and homework review at the beginning of class usually means that new concepts aren't introduced until close to the middle of class, when the brain is entering a low trough. It's not that students can't learn during this time; it's just more cumbersome. It makes sense: the brain is fresh at the beginning of a lesson, and the working memory can easily handle the amount of information coming in. By mid-class, however, the brain has reached its limit to chunk information, so the brain has more difficulty retaining it all. Trying to learn something new at this point is a steeper climb. Toward the end of class, the brain is apt to pick up some speed again, as students begin sorting out the concepts covered (Sousa, 2008). Because students are making sense of the new concepts and beginning to demonstrate understanding, the close of class also presents a good opportunity for formative assessment.

Too often, a class begins with a warm-up that ties up brains with review work and lower-level thinking, underutilizing students' brainpower. Tacking homework review onto that time continues to push new learning back, and the clock ticks away until one-third of the class time has expired and students are restless and disinterested—just in time for the new content.

Knowing that the optimal time for grasping information is in those powerful opening minutes, rethinking warm-ups is essential—especially for students at risk of failure.

Why Success Starters Work

Think about the last time you had dinner at a restaurant. How long did you remember the name of the server? Probably not long. After entering a friend's contact number into your cell phone, how long does your brain retain it? Most likely, just a few seconds.

Where does all this information go? Most of it gets deleted by the brain. Our brains can't save everything, so they have to be selective. Your brain evaluated the importance of hanging on to the server's name and remembering your friend's phone number and decided that it was unnecessary information. Similarly, students' brains are deleting information all day long. If the brain decides that a piece of information is unimportant, it holds it for only around 30 seconds before dropping it (Sousa, 2008). Scary news for students and teachers, but it's good to know as we go about planning lessons.

Clearly, it is beneficial to the learning process when students find a new concept interesting and relevant right from the start. Information that is compelling, is novel, or has value to the learner is more likely to be processed and stored. If the activity is hands-on, that's even better for retention (Willis, 2006). During the opening minutes of class, students' brains are making decisions about the importance and interest level of the material and determining students' level of involvement. If the material isn't interesting to students, their brains will likely tune out or quickly delete the new information. Although students need routines in their school day, predictable sameness lowers the brain's interest (Sousa, 2008). If everything is the same every day, there is no need for the brain to adapt (Jensen, 2005).

Beginning class with immediately engaging material is especially important for underperforming learners who are on the verge of nonparticipation. Jensen (2005) explains that students' perception that a task bears little relevance or interest to them negatively affects student motivation. Asking a struggling student to expend effort on something that seems irrelevant or tedious is a tough climb. In contrast, getting students actively, genuinely engaged in something they deem meaningful sets up an environment for increased, sustained participation and productivity. Thoughtful openers that tap into students' interests are a mainstay in gifted classrooms, but they are needed in every classroom, for every lesson.

"Do I Have What It Takes?"

At the same time students are determining whether a task will be interesting and relevant, their brains are also deciding just how much they are willing to risk. For academically vulnerable students, taking a risk and failing hurts more than not trying at all. Students are wondering, "Is the water safe for jumping in, or should I stay on the edge of the pool?" They are more likely to dive in academically if they believe success is possible.

Success at learning something new largely depends on the brain's ability to connect it to prior knowledge. Prior knowledge is where the learning begins (Jensen, 2005). Connecting new information to prior knowledge facilitates the processing of information so that rather than getting lost or deleted, new learning makes it to the brain's long-term storage area (Willis, 2006).

Most educators are aware of the tremendous importance of prior knowledge. The challenge is that every student has a different set of prior knowledge "files" in his or her brain. Some folders are thick and complete, whereas others are thin and skimpy. Students probably know more than they realize, however. During the opening minutes, you can use success starters to access and fatten up students' prior knowledge files, signaling to students that this new concept is, in fact, attainable.

Implementing Success Starters

We have established that a class's opening minutes are the most fertile time for learning: students' brains are wide-open, ready, and making decisions—without students' awareness, really—about their level of interest and engagement. Brains are deciding quickly whether to keep information or toss it. Thus, the effectiveness of the lesson largely depends on the instructional strategies used in these precious opening minutes.

When I collaborate with teachers on constructing these openers, we begin by determining the real-world relevance of the standard. Students are smart to ask, "Why are we learning this?" Effective instruction dictates, however, that we resolve that question in the opener before they even ask. This process can be challenging at first. It may seem difficult, for example, to discern the relevance of the defeat of the Spanish Armada to students' lives. But the rise of one empire and the decline of another and the role of underdogs in overcoming obstacles to secure a victory are both powerful narratives. (Plus, blood, guts, and sinking ships can be an exhilarating way to start class!) If the day's topic is crustaceans, class could begin with the perusal of a menu from a local seafood restaurant or a video clip of fishermen bringing in their catch of crab or lobster. If the lesson is on *To Kill a Mockingbird*, the real-world hook may be about taking a stand against injustice. If the standard addresses trade deficits in the economy, an intriguing start could be collecting data from students' shirts and shoes to calculate the percentage of items manufactured in the United States. And so on.

Effective success starters vary lesson by lesson. As compelling and riveting as possible, these activities spark authentic involvement rather than compliance. They aim to set students up for success in mastering the learning objective of the lesson. When constructing this portion of the lesson, keep in mind the following criteria. Success starters should

- Connect to prior knowledge.
- Hold high interest, real-world relevance, and value for students.
- Be explicitly tied to the standard being taught.
- Engage every learner.
- Answer the question "What's this got to do with me?"
- Be fast-paced and time-conscious.
- Set up the lesson, including the purpose for any assigned reading.
- When appropriate, employ concrete representations before abstract concepts.

Strategies for Effective Success Starters

The examples in the following sections can be modified for many concepts and aim to spark your thinking about constructing success starters. These strategies, from role-playing to questioning, have been used in countless classrooms with great success. However, every concept you teach poses unique opportunities for stimulating student involvement and thinking right out of the gate.

Role-Playing

With role-playing, you can take a concept that is far removed from students and make it about them. The following examples illustrate how openers that incorporate role-playing foster critical thinking, provide relevance, and engage student interest.

Example: Jamestown Colony. Every student studies the formation of the Jamestown Colony at least once in his or her academic career. This is a topic potentially very low in student interest and relevance. If asked to summarize it, a student might reply, "Over 400 years ago, a bunch of men in weird clothes boarded a ship from somewhere looking for gold, and things didn't work out too well."

But wait—what if the *students* were the leaders of this dangerous expedition? What decisions would they make about the colony? What if they compared their decisions with those of the expedition's historic leaders? This opener, ideal for upper-elementary students and middle schoolers, facilitates critical thinking about what actually goes into starting a colony:

> You are the leaders of a dangerous new expedition. You will be traveling on a long journey to a potentially threatening land and will have to overcome many obstacles, such as food and water shortages, lack of housing, and disease. Whom you select (by occupation) to join you on this risky venture is up to you. Think about the jobs that will be required once you arrive. You have five minutes for this task. (Hint: wouldn't it be helpful if some had talents in more than one area? For example, a carpenter with a knack for cooking?)

Note that teachers can tweak this activity for younger students by providing a list of occupations and having students check off which ones they believe would be the most needed in starting a colony.

After students, working in groups, make decisions about their initial settlers, the teacher provides a primary source—a ship's log—showing who actually came to Jamestown. Students will be surprised to discover that over half of the original settlers were men who had no occupation and that historians are still debating how much these early decisions negatively affected the colony. This rich context provides a deeper understanding of the hardships at the colony, and seeing actual names on a real ship's log personalizes the harsh fate many met. In addition, this activity satisfies one of the Common Core standards on examining primary sources (CCSS.ELA-Literacy.RH.6-8.2).

Example: How diseases spread. Role-playing can take many forms, but one common denominator is that students are in charge. This shift of control onto their shoulders boosts motivation. The following scenario is a nod to Dr. John Snow, a fascinating disease detective from the 1800s who saved countless lives by discovering that cholera was being spread by a single London water pump. The purpose of this opener is to get students thinking about how diseases spread. This opener would best suit middle or high school students, but role-playing works well for students at all grade levels.

You are the chief doctor of a university's health department, and you are facing a medical emergency in the community. Lives depend on the actions you take. As you read the timeline, create a list of questions you will ask and tools you will need to solve the mystery. Here is the developing situation that you must address:

2:50 a.m.: Two male students living in a fraternity house are rushed to the hospital. Police interviews reveal that they had attended a football game at Sanford Stadium the night before. One reportedly went out on the town after the game. A witness reported that both had been up all night with stomach cramps and vomiting.

4:00 a.m.: A student phones 911 for an ambulance. She felt fine until she ate a late-night snack after working in the chemistry building. She was suddenly stricken with severe diarrhea, chills, and disorientation.

4:15 a.m.: A 65-year-old food-service worker at the student center is found dead in the kitchen by coworkers. No other information is yet available.

4:30 a.m.: Two coaches from the opposing team are admitted to the hospital with severe dehydration.

4:35 a.m.: A jogger collapses in front of Memorial Hall. No other information is available at this time.

4:45 a.m.: Panic is beginning to spread. Parents and reporters are calling and demanding answers.

Questions you will ask (and of whom):

Tools you need:

Both these role-plays meet the criteria for effective success starters: by allowing students to make decisions, they establish relevance and have a high level of interest. In addition, they engage students in critical thinking, prime students' prior knowledge, are fast-paced, and set up the lesson to follow.

Surveys

A quick scan of magazine covers reveals the popularity of surveys. *Are you a good friend? What's your personality type?* Many of us enjoy running through such quiz questions and scoring ourselves using the key provided, which usually reveals that we are even better at something than we had imagined.

Surveys also work well in the classroom, both as openers and as quick formative assessments. A survey immediately answers the brain's question "What does this have to do with me?" Surveys can be used for just about any topic. For example, you can open a lesson on the Great Depression with questions like "Have you ever had to move to a new place?" and "Have you known someone who has lost his or her job?" Or for a standard on the respiratory system, ask students, "Have you ever had a cold?" or "Do you know someone with allergies?"

Example: Inherited traits. In this scenario, as a class embarks on a standard on inherited traits, students fill out a survey querying them about their own genetic traits (see Figure 3.1). Although this example is

---

FIGURE 3.1
Inherited Traits Survey

1. Can you curl your tongue?	____YES	____NO
2. Is your second toe longer than your big toe?	____YES	____NO
3. Can you make "Vulcan" hands?	____YES	____NO
4. Are your earlobes attached at the bottom?	____YES	____NO
5. Do you have a "hitchhiker thumb"?	____YES	____NO
6. Do you have dimples?	____YES	____NO
7. Fold your hands: is your right thumb on top?	____YES	____NO

most suitable for elementary school students, it can readily be tweaked for older ones.

After students take the survey, the teacher collects and shares classroom data: how many sets of dimples are in the classroom? How many attached versus free earlobes do we have?

This survey primes students' prior knowledge, is fast-paced, and sets up the lesson to follow. In addition, it establishes relevance for students, who love exploring their own characteristics. Because of their high level of interest, surveys typically get 100 percent participation, which starts every student off with success.

Prediction

Prediction openers ask students to anticipate what will occur in a story, a science lab, or an economic situation. Predicting involves thinking about what you know and applying it to a new situation. Sorts work well for prediction and are hands-on, which promotes engagement.

Example: Prediction sort (math). To kick off a lesson on integers, this opener has students work with partners to sort responses into two piles: positive and negative. Before the lesson, the teacher cuts the paper strips, places them in small plastic bags, and shakes them up, ready for students to sort. Figure 3.2 shows a completed integer sort.

Example: Prediction sort (science). Sorts can take many forms. The sort shown in Figure 3.3 contains a scrambled assortment of facts and myths about earthquakes. Students must predict what is true and not true and place each statement in the appropriate column. All the teacher

FIGURE 3.2 **Integer Sort (Sorted)**	
Positive	**Negative**
profit	loss
deposit check in bank	withdraw cash at ATM
bonus points	items missed on test
up	down
average temperature in Hawaii	average temperature in Antarctica

FIGURE 3.3
Earthquake Sort (Unsorted)

True	False
Seismology is the study of earthquakes.	Earthquakes are caused by friction between giant plates of rock.
Residents near the Atlantic Coast are the Americans most vulnerable to earthquakes.	Scientists can accurately predict earthquakes so that residents will have days to prepare.
Earthquakes vary widely in strength.	The earth is not alone in experiencing quakes; in fact, the moon has similar waves called *moonquakes.*
During an earthquake, you should immediately take cover close to a building or under a tree.	The epicenter of an earthquake is located on the earth's surface directly above the starting point.
The strength of earthquakes cannot be measured.	Some evidence indicates that animals can predict earthquakes.

needs to do is cut the chart into strips and let students go to work! As the lesson progresses, students continually check their sorts and reposition their strips to correct misconceptions. Were their predictions accurate? Why or why not?

Sorts are incredibly versatile, engaging tools that have numerous variations, such as the grab bag. For example, before reading a fictional text about a family going through hard financial times, groups of students can separate items out of a grab bag, determining which ones are more likely to belong to the family on a tight budget (e.g., *vacation* versus *staycation*, or *roast beef* versus *beans*). In science, students might predict types of matter by items in the grab bag, which might contain a blown-up balloon, a wooden block, and a bottle of shampoo. In health, students can rank-order foods from highest to lowest level of nutrition.

The tactile nature of sorts works well with all students, who tend to jump right in to the activity. The element of suspense is also a motivator: students are eager to learn if their responses were correct. On occasions when time does not permit a sort, anticipation guides are a good substitute.

Example: Anticipation guide. In this example, students predict which items are sources of electromagnetic radiation and consider which would have the lowest and highest amounts (see Figure 3.4).

All these prediction openers satisfy the criteria for effective success starters: they are relevant and hold high interest, soliciting students' opinions and knowledge (sorts, in particular, typically get 100 percent participation); are fast-paced; prime the prior knowledge pump; and neatly segue into the lesson.

Questioning

What do you want to know about cell phones? About the Holocaust? About parasites? Odds are, what you're curious about will differ in some ways from what others want to know (or think you should know). The strategy of questioning accords with our tendency to be more curious about questions that we came up with than about questions assigned to us. How much more engaging and provocative is it to think deeply about what you want to know about a topic than to research answers to textbook-generated questions? With questioning, exploring the answers to students' questions becomes the lesson's purpose, and learning becomes authentic.

FIGURE 3.4

Anticipation Guide: Electromagnetic Radiation

Place a check next to the items that you think are sources of electromagnetic radiation. Now predict which of the items you checked have the lowest amounts, and which have the highest (write *L* for low and *H* for high). What thinking led to your decisions?

____ 1. Tanning bed	____ 8. Dental X-rays
____ 2. Cell phone	____ 9. Microwave oven
____ 3. Radon	____ 10. Laptop computer
____ 4. Airport X-rays	____ 11. Desk lamp
____ 5. Radio	____ 12. Fireflies
____ 6. CT scans	____ 13. Skin
____ 7. Rays from outer space	____ 14. Fluorescent light bulbs

Example: Question sun. This is a simple yet highly effective approach to generating questions. First, draw a sun with rays on the board, placing the topic in the center. Then model the process by posing a question you have about the topic: "I want to know if snakes mate for life. What do *you* want to know about snakes?" As the questioning proceeds, categorization emerges (e.g., "Let's put questions about live births and eggs over here with reproduction"). Figure 3.5 shows an in-progress question sun on snakes.

A question sun can set up a lesson beautifully, and the best part is, it's entirely student-created. Every student has *some* knowledge about snakes, and the class generates what it wants to learn about during the lesson. Although first-time implementation should be with the whole group, once students are comfortable with the process they can work in small groups to create their own question suns and then share them with the class.

A bonus of this strategy is that students continue to answer their questions as the lesson or reading progresses. Students will generate certain questions (some of them outlandish) that the initial lesson will not expressly answer, such as "Can snakes have twins?" That's a good thing! Their job is now to independently research answers to questions not answered in class and report back.

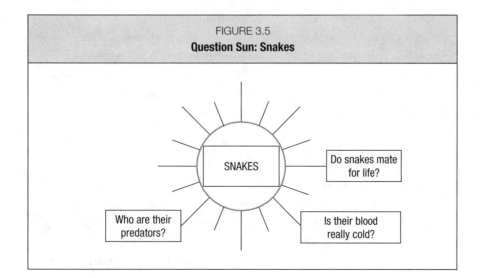

FIGURE 3.5
Question Sun: Snakes

Example: Question starter cards. Question starter cards are an equally effective way to generate student questioning. First, create index cards containing question words (e.g., *would, will, how,* and *why*) that will guide students toward the learning objective. Then students divide into groups, deal the cards face down, and "play cards," coming up with questions for the group cued by the cards they are dealt. The questions will vary depending on the topic; questions for a character analysis would look different from questions about causes of a war.

For example, counselors may use question starter cards to teach students how to cope with mistakes and see them as learning experiences. A student who plays the *what* card might ask, "What should I do if I make a mistake in class?" whereas the student who gets the *how* card might ask, "How can mistakes help me learn?" and the student who gets the *why* card could ask, "Why do I get embarrassed when I make a mistake?" In a unit on weather, students may ask one another, "How do tornadoes start?" "When are tornadoes most likely to occur?" and "What should I do if I see a tornado?"

One benefit of question starter cards is that they cue all students to engage in questioning, even the most reluctant participants, in a safe way. Plus, they're versatile: teachers can use question starter cards as openers to infuse novelty and interest, and later in class as a type of formative assessment. In addition, cards can be shuffled and redistributed for additional question-and-answer sessions.

Rather than jumping into a lesson ("We're going to study amphibians now"), questioning openers pull inquiries from the recesses of students' minds and spark meaning and relevance. They activate not only students' prior knowledge but also their curiosity about a topic. There aren't too many better ways to set up a lesson!

Brainstorming

An explosion of rapid-fire thoughts channeled into a structure is an apt description of the following two brainstorming strategies, which have every student actively thinking and sharing. The number-one rule of brainstorming is *safety first:* no criticism of others' ideas. By the nature of the process, some answers will land off-target, but that's part of the fun: during a brainstorming session, you'll often hear laughter erupt as students share their crazy, creative, wonderful responses.

Example: Splash-sort-label. In this exercise, which works well from upper-elementary school through high school, brainstorming meets critical thinking meets classification. It begins with individual ideas. Provide each student with 10 or so sticky notes (cut-up recycled paper will also work). Then announce the topic—for example, "Tell me everything you know about *government.*" Next, give students two minutes to individually write down their responses, one thought per sticky note. During this short period, students fly through their sticky notes, recording answers like *licenses, courts, vetoes, impeachment, president, governor, traffic tickets, Supreme Court,* and *taxes.*

Now, students form groups and combine their sticky notes. On a section of the wall, students "splash" their answers (see Figure 3.6) and

---

FIGURE 3.6
Splash-Sort-Label Wall

then step back to survey their groups' responses. There will be some repetition, so groups remove redundant notes as needed. Next, group members collaboratively come up with categories and headings that fit their responses and rearrange sticky notes into those categories. In the lesson on government, for example, groups could create categories such as *local, state,* and *federal* and generate a heading that reads "Opinions About Government."

Finally, groups share their work with the class or a nearby group. After this sharing, the teacher begins teaching the new material. At the end of the lesson, students can revisit their original thoughts and decide what should be added to their groups' splash-sort-label walls.

Example: Alpha brainstorming. Alpha brainstorming is a brain dump that you can use as an opener and then revisit to conclude the lesson. Have students form groups, and provide each one with a chart similar to the one in Figure 3.7. Each group will need to assign a recorder.

FIGURE 3.7 **Alpha Brainstorming**					
A	B	C	D	E	F
G	H	I	J	K	L
M	N	O	P	Q	R
S	T	U	V	W	X
Y	Z				

(I typically recommend that recorders should be the fastest writers, not necessarily the students with the best handwriting!) After giving students a question or prompt (e.g., "Write down everything you know about outer space"), they get four to five minutes to come up with an answer for each letter of the alphabet. The goal is to get at least one response for each letter, but you can tweak the activity to suit your class's needs. For example, if you teach younger students or don't want the activity to take up too much time, consider assigning the first half of the alphabet to one side of the room and the second half to the other. For more difficult letters, such as *X*, you may want to allow students to use words that merely contain the letter rather than start with it. Once groups have finished, they share their responses with the rest of the class.

Both splash-sort-label and alpha brainstorming typically get 100 percent student participation, so students kick off the lesson with success. Students are asked to share their opinions, ideas, and knowledge, which creates a high degree of interest and relevance. The special beauty of brainstorming is that, as students pool their prior knowledge, those who had scant knowledge of the topic just learned enough to connect to new learning. Finally, like all the strategies discussed in this section, the openers are fast-paced and set up the lesson to follow.

Concrete Representations

Abstract concepts can be tough for students to grasp, so a good way to ease students into them is to use openers that model concrete representations of the concept. This practice helps students systematically progress to the next level of thinking. In math and science, for example, working with manipulatives such as blocks, play money, and measuring devices before jumping into abstract concepts can strengthen student processing.

Across all subject areas, showing pictures during the opening portion of a lesson can help students develop context. The Great Depression, for example, is a far-removed concept for most students, so a teacher might want to open a lesson on this topic with a compelling slideshow of photos from the period and have students jot down their impressions. Graphs, images, and maps can work well in all subjects and all grades, whether the subject is weather, phases of the moon, geometric shapes in architecture, angles in a junkyard, fashions of a time period, or tire pressure. After the lesson, students can revisit the opening representations through the lens of what they have learned.

Teachers can also use picture books to establish context, fill in gaps in prior knowledge, and spur interest. Inexpensive picture books are available for all content areas and grade levels. There's a common misconception that picture books are just for younger students, but there are many compelling ones aimed at adolescents. These not only serve as engaging openers but also can be used effectively throughout the course of a lesson.

Working Around Administrative and Logistical Challenges

The opening minutes are so vital for students that they require a high degree of instructional protection. I hope you see the power of success starters, especially in comparison with classroom warm-ups. However, if teachers in your building are expected to use warm-ups or bell ringers for administrative purposes, transitioning to success starters may present some difficulties. It may be valuable to open up a building-level conversation about the prioritization and placement of administrative tasks. For example, water breaks and office summons are best reserved for the middle part of class. On the other hand, taking attendance immediately may be nonnegotiable, deemed critical for accountability. Fortunately, teachers can accomplish this task with engaging openers: all the openers in this chapter get students started right away so that teachers can take attendance while engaging work is under way.

If the administration decides to retain schoolwide warm-ups, it is imperative to at least have a conversation about the amount of time allotted for them. Rather than post five review questions or problems, for example, consider moving to one or two, so that new instruction gets started in a more timely fashion.

In addition, find some ways to provide students with feedback about homework without sacrificing new learning. Here are some strategies I have found helpful:

• When students enter the room, have them place a dot on a number line that corresponds with the homework question that gave them the most difficulty. This creates a bar graph of responses. To guide them, ask, "If we have just enough time to talk about one part of the homework, what would it be?" Select the top two items and review those.

• Write the numbers of the homework questions on the board and have students draw a tally mark under the two they would most like to discuss.

• Have students place homework on the corner of their desks. During the student work period—the large middle chunk of class in which students work collaboratively or practice independently—review homework and provide feedback.

• In a co-taught class, one teacher can collect homework and give it a quick check for common misconceptions. Then the teachers can provide feedback at the most opportune moment in class.

A common logistical issue that can impede the effectiveness of the opening minutes is dealing with students who lack the supplies they need for work. My observations in hundreds of classrooms reveal—and every teacher on the face of the earth will concur—that the same students who are struggling in class are often the ones without a pencil or paper. We can make ourselves crazy lecturing them about responsibility, or we can just give them a pencil so that they can learn. I strongly advocate the latter approach. My hope is that, as students realize some success, they become more likely to come prepared for class. Having a system in place can alleviate stress on both sides of the issue. To avoid emptying your own pockets, sign out supplies to students, provide scrappy ones found in hallways, or purchase cheap golf pencils that do the job. In this way, learning can begin with positive connections and compelling learning, not a battle over a 10-cent pencil.

Reflections on Success Starters

After a recent professional development session that I facilitated, a teacher shared her experience in a way that encapsulated the problems with warm-ups. She said she was spending a great deal of time on warm-ups because of the many common misconceptions students held. After the warm-up, she would tackle the previous night's homework, which also took a great deal of time owing to students' difficulties with the material. By the time the teacher was done teaching the *new* material, time was so short that students had inadequate time to practice new concepts. As a result, they came to class the next day with misconceptions and homework problems—again. Hands on her hips, the teacher exclaimed, "I've gotten myself into a cycle, haven't I?"

Student success—or failure—begins when a lesson does. Moviemakers know that the opening minutes of a film need to be compelling to hold viewers' interests: car chases and foot races across rooftops keep our eyes glued to the screen. In the same way a viewer flips through TV channels looking for something interesting, learners' brains are deciding during the opening minutes if the lesson matters to them. Will students grab hold or tune out? Students are also weighing their likelihood of success. If there is a good chance of success, they will exert more effort. Students who are at risk of failing, however, are less likely to participate if the balance is not in their favor. The risk of embarrassment and loss of face to peers is a high price to pay.

Our knowledge of how students' brains operate and of the decisions being made in the opening minutes of class should influence the way we teach. If we want students to stay in the fast lane, they need to realize right away that (a) this is interesting, (b) this matters to me, and (c) I think I can do this! The openers described in this chapter immediately engage every student, and every learner can find success in them. That doesn't mean they are easy or low-level; on the contrary, they activate prior knowledge, stimulate critical thinking, and foster collaboration. Best of all, after the opener, students' brains are excited about learning and ready to receive, process, and retain new information.

Checklist for success starters:

- ❏ Students' intellectual curiosity is piqued in the opening minutes of class.
- ❏ The activity makes real-world connections and is relevant to students.
- ❏ The activity fosters higher-order thinking.
- ❏ The activity enables all students to achieve success in the opening minutes.
- ❏ The activity is tightly linked to the lesson's learning goal.

4

Formative Assessment and Feedback: Checking Student Understanding Minute by Minute

A riveting opener has piqued students' intellectual curiosity and tapped into their prior knowledge. Today's learning goal has been clearly established. Students are primed to explore the standard. The lesson is off to a great start!

Toward the end of class, the teacher carefully collects student work and places it in organizing bins. At the end of the day, she gathers up all the papers from the bins and zips them into a satchel, then safely locks the satchel into the trunk of her car. The papers then get driven around for a few days. The teacher eventually retrieves the papers from the trunk to make room for groceries and moves them to the dining table. A couple more days pass. Finally, during a rerun of *Friends,* the assessment process begins. *Xs,* checkmarks, and occasionally profound comments in scented magic marker adorn the pages.

The papers (minus the few the cat destroyed) make the trek back to school via the satchel and the trunk and land in a bin marked "graded."

"I've got your papers graded," the teacher announces with relief, half-expecting the news media to document this momentous occasion.

Confused looks come to some students' faces. "When did we do this?" they ask, rustling through the papers. "I think this kid moved away," another student helpfully observes. Some students immediately wad or shred their papers and toss them toward the trash bin. A few let the papers linger on their desks for all to see, wondering whether their refrigerator will accommodate any more glory.

The Trouble with Testing and Grades

Struggling learners, research finds, often have a rockier relationship with graded tests than do their more successful peers. Low marks on tests can confirm their perception of themselves as academic failures and tend to lead to a decline in motivation and engagement (Davies, 2007). Students may decide that the risk of failure is too high to continue making an effort. These students don't see a low grade as a potential path toward progress but rather as a testament to their current value as a student. Stiggins (2004) cautions that students may evaluate their own potential for success on the basis of test scores. Low grades can actually perpetuate failure by providing concrete "proof" of students' academic losing streak.

On the other hand, higher-achieving students are more likely to perceive grades as fair and even enjoy receiving grades. Not coincidentally, research (Harlen & Crick, 2003) shows that successful students tend to demonstrate more perseverance during tests, have more-positive self-perceptions, and are better at taking tests than lower-achieving students.

As teachers, we may see giving grades as just part of our work routine, but students often take grades quite personally. We have all seen frustrated learners immediately destroy the evidence of their poor performance by tearing or crumpling up their graded papers.

Seeing as grades and high-stakes testing aren't going anywhere, how can we improve this situation? How can we build academic capacity in weaker students as standards and tests continue to increase in rigor?

Why Formative Assessment and Feedback Work

As it turns out, one of the best ways to improve low-achieving students' academic performance and summative assessment scores is to administer frequent *ungraded* assessments for formative purposes that focus on helping students learn rather than measure what they already learned (or didn't learn). Black and Wiliam (1998) explain that students in classrooms rich with formative assessment can learn in six or seven months what would take other students an entire year to learn. Indeed, studies have indicated that formative assessment is comparable to one-on-one tutoring in its effectiveness (Stiggins, 2004). Further, these gains in achievement can be sustained over extended periods and translate to greater student success on externally mandated standardized tests (Leahy et al., 2005).

Formative assessment achieves such strong gains because it provides a vehicle to give students timely feedback on their work and enables teachers to make immediate adjustments to instruction. When the frequency of descriptive feedback goes up and evaluative feedback goes down, students learn more (Davies, 2007). Hattie and Timperley (2007) reported that feedback has potentially great power in influencing student achievement, particularly when it is about how to perform a task more effectively.

The use of formative assessment is especially effective in improving the achievement of low-performing students (Stiggins, 2004). The feedback generated by ongoing, highly visible formative assessment holds great power for transforming low achievers into successful students. Within feedback-driven environments, students begin to hit learning targets and realize continual small successes. As a result, they become more likely to persevere when they *don't* succeed the first time around (Stiggins, 2004), and rather than viewing standards as unattainable and futile, they become more confident learners.

If we want students to meet learning goals the first time and remain in the fast lane, they and their teachers must know exactly where they stand on the content being taught—not just at the end of the week or even at the end of class, but right now. Teachers must be aware of students' progress minute by minute, so that they can provide timely feedback and help close gaps in understanding.

Implementing Instructional Feedback

Although feedback holds great promise for helping students reach their learning goals, not all feedback is created equal. It is beneficial to examine what kinds of feedback do *not* produce results.

For example, artificial or undeserved praise should be avoided (Pajares, 2006). In our eagerness to encourage struggling students, it can be tempting to heap praise on them just to keep them in the game. When it's not based on real evidence of progress, however, this praise can undermine trust and embarrass a student. Students know when praise is deserved.

Similar to praise, teachers often use rewards such as candy and stickers in an attempt to encourage students to complete tasks. Perhaps surprisingly, however, rewards (and punishments) are one of the least effective ways to increase student achievement (Hattie & Timperley, 2007).

Finally, feedback that doesn't focus specifically on the work or provide any guidance is also counterproductive. Clymer and Wiliam (2007) reported that feedback focused on the person rather than the task can actually cause a decline in student performance. Simply telling students whether their responses were right or wrong can also have a negative effect on learning; instead, students benefit from explanations and feedback that show them how they can improve and encourage them to continue working hard (Marzano et al., 2001).

Now that we have cleared the table of ineffective feedback practices, how can we supply *effective* feedback? Providing effective feedback, particularly to struggling students, can be challenging; it requires skill, tenacity, clear vision, and diplomacy. Students in a failure pattern may be defensive or feel embarrassed about the frequent presence of a teacher at their desk. In fact, some struggling learners do not seek assistance at all (Hattie & Timperley, 2007) but exhibit self-protection behaviors, brushing off attempts of assistance with comments like "I've got it" or even "This is so easy." These may be the same students who did not complete their homework, have been absent for three days, and came to class without paper or pencil. The following six research-based principles of effective feedback will enable you to navigate these obstacles and help students realize success at their learning tasks.

Principle 1: Establish clear, specific learning goals at the onset of the lesson. Learning begins with a goal. Learning goals must be explicit, consistent, and clearly articulated at the beginning of the lesson and throughout learning. Although this principle is important for all students, it speaks specifically to lower-achieving students, who may fail to understand even what is required of them (Black & Wiliam, 1998).

Learning goals should be stated in student-friendly terms, and it bears repeating that simply taping standards on a wall is inadequate. Students need (and deserve) a clear, stationary target toward which they can strive and against which they can gauge their progress.

I advocate creating a concept map with clearly stated learning goals that crescendo toward the central enduring understanding (see Figure 2.1, p. 27). This format breaks up standards' text into understandable, attainable chunks. Whichever format you choose, understand that classroom success begins with an explicit goal, and that conversations, lessons, student work, and assessment should be designed to enable students to reach these goals.

Principle 2: Provide feedback that demonstrates explicitly how students can achieve the learning goal. The purpose of instructional feedback is to improve students' performance—to close gaps between their current level of understanding and the learning goals. From the moment the teacher articulates the learning goal, the teaching process transforms from simply delivering information to openly gathering evidence of progress. If students' learning goal is to be able to describe the digestive system, feedback must narrow specifically to that goal. Straying into feedback on handwriting, grammatical errors, or tardiness can derail the feedback process and cloud the true purpose of today's work.

Feedback is about the standard, not the student. It's not personal; it's about making work stronger. As students begin to see that feedback is helping them improve their performance, they develop more trust in the process and eventually realize that errors and misunderstandings are a critical part of the learning process. Effective feedback has the power to build academic traction in students whose wheels have been spinning for too long.

Principle 3: Involve all learners in the feedback process. Placing full responsibility for feedback duties with teachers not only is an inefficient use of time but also cuts students out of a vital learning process. If teachers employ the three tiers of teacher, self, and peer feedback, however, all students can get the feedback they need to move forward right now.

From the moment a concept or standard's learning goals have been articulated, students themselves become collectors of evidence of learning—that is, they become involved in assessing their own learning. Self-assessment shifts ownership of learning onto students' shoulders and promotes greater collaboration between teachers and students. In addition, Shepard (2000) contends, self-evaluation can lead to increased interest in the actual learning and less focus on grades. Students who engage in self-assessment over time see that success is possible if they continue to strive; the evidence they collect provides them with opportunities to share the "story of their success" (Stiggins, 2004, p. 27). Students can use rubrics, answer keys, and finished work samples to evaluate their own progress against the learning objective.

Peers helping one another understand the concept or standard also move learning forward (Leahy et al., 2005). By actively incorporating peer feedback, teachers can multiply the impact of feedback (Davies, 2007). For example, a teacher of a class of 30 students who travels from desk to desk to examine each student's work individually is not making the best use of class time. First, the desk-to-desk model does not provide adequate time for meaningful feedback conversations. In addition, odds are that some students will need more than one visit, so while the teacher is visiting her 23rd student, several previously seen students may have their hands up, requesting further assistance. To start using peer feedback, encourage students to form pairs or small groups and examine one another's work. Students could, for example,

- Compare whiteboard responses with a partner and reach consensus on the correct answers.
- Compare sticky-note summaries of a reading passage.
- Peer-edit one another's writing assignments.
- Compare lab results and examine the differences.

Principle 4: Deliver feedback as immediately and frequently as possible. There is a positive correlation between the frequency of formative assessment and student achievement (Marzano, 2007). For low-achieving students in particular, frequent and immediate feedback is imperative. Allowing struggling students to linger in doubt about how to correctly complete a task is a recipe for frustration and failure. Especially in the early stages of learning, when errors are more common, immediate error correction results in faster rates of knowledge acquisition (Hattie & Timperley, 2007). Conversely, practicing something incorrectly can result in increased academic unraveling, as students' misconceptions become further entrenched.

As a teacher, I always found it frustrating when visitors arrived in my classroom on learning walks, proceeded to write furiously on clipboards, and vanished once they were done, without ever saying a word. "What did they write down?" I would wonder. "Is there something I could do better? Was it great? Was it horrible? Am I going to get fired?" Students, too, want to know before they continue on the wrong path, "Am I doing this right? Is my topic sentence OK?"

Principle 5: Link academic progress to controllable factors, such as hard work and tenacity. One of the most notable differences between low and high achievers is their belief system about how people become successful in school. Mendler (2000) observes that successful students tend to believe that hard work is the key to success. In contrast, lower-achieving students are more likely to hold that success emanates from innate ability rather than effort. Sadly, struggling learners tend to perceive themselves as academically incapable. When teachers implore them to work harder, they may think, "If I am not smart enough to do it, what will harder work accomplish?" To further complicate the issue, Margolis and McCabe (2006) note, struggling learners tend to believe that needing to work hard is a sign of low ability and personal inadequacy. All these beliefs can inhibit students' academic progress.

It's important for teachers to recognize that students will work harder when they believe that they, rather than outside forces, have control over their academic results (Protheroe, 2010). We must send the message to our lower-achieving students that diligence, hard work, and academic achievement are controllable factors and that students are not stuck in their current spot; rather, their success is largely within their control and is quite changeable.

Accordingly, when you deliver feedback to students, it is important to link effort and tenacity with success. You can reinforce this by saying things like "Your perseverance on this problem is commendable; it's a tough one that requires some tenacity," or "I see the hard work that you have put in, and your outline shows the result of those efforts."

Principle 6: Be as encouraging as is genuinely possible. When you give feedback, your tone should communicate optimism and helpfulness, not blame or judgment. Where grades can deflate, feedback can inspire. Feedback lays out a map of next steps that students can take to continue moving toward their goals. Feedback has the power to keep students in the game.

With students who are behind and have widespread areas of weakness in their work, it is important to be selective about feedback. When observing a sea of errors, maintaining a strict focus on the learning goal can help keep feedback manageable for both teacher and students.

Sometimes, the students who need the most frequent feedback are those who want it the least. The seemingly constant presence of the teacher at their desk can draw undue attention to their situation. It is important for weaker learners in particular to recognize that conversations with their teachers are productive, safe, and aimed at advancing their learning. The feedback conversation will go more smoothly if you start with something positive: in almost any sample of student work, you should be able to find some aspect to commend before discussing next steps. This can reduce defensiveness so that students are more open to changes. For example,

- "Your use of transitions is commendable. Are there other transition words that might add more variety to your writing?"
- "It is evident that you understand how to properly line up decimals. Now let's look at how you arrived at your answer."
- "I want to commend your use of citing evidence in the first paragraph. What might strengthen the second paragraph?"
- "I applaud the example you gave of nonrenewable resources. Now, the standard is asking us to compare nonrenewable with renewable resources, so can you think of some ways in which the two types of resources are similar and different?"

Formative Assessment Strategies

To give immediate feedback, we need to be able to see student progress right now, in this moment. Performance-arena examples of feedback and formative assessment can provide helpful models for classroom teachers.

A band teacher, for example, can hear right away when the flutists are off on their timing and stop them immediately, provide corrective feedback, model the movement, and listen to them again. She may pair a proficient student with one who is not quite there. Metronome in hand, the pair proceeds to a practice room to work through the rough spots until the struggling student has improved. This feedback spurs progress toward the learning goal and ensures success in the summative assessment: the spring concert.

Similarly, a baseball coach who observes errors in the pitcher's form during practice does not storm the mound with a grade book and a red pen. Instead, he meets with the pitcher and the catcher, and they have a conversation loaded with feedback about how the pitcher can meet the target. The pitcher adjusts his technique, throws some practice balls, and continually makes changes based on ongoing feedback. Without this intervention, the player may not perform well on the summative assessment—the game.

It is decidedly more challenging to determine exactly where students are in the academic arena. There are no tennis balls smashing into nets or screeching violins to cue the teacher on which issues need to be addressed. Instead, teachers are powering through a packed curriculum in a classroom crammed with students slumped over filler paper. It may seem as though almost every student has "gotten" it—until the teacher examines students' papers later. By that time, the learning goal has passed, students have left the building, and the optimal time for correction is gone.

Although definitions for formative assessment abound, I like Popham's (2008) description of it as a *process* conducted during instruction that yields feedback enabling teachers and students to make adjustments that improve student achievement. Formative assessment does not need to be conducted through traditional paper-and-pencil activities. In fact, some of the most effective assessments do not resemble tests at all, a bonus for academically fragile students. Indeed, assessments used for formative purposes can be some of the most engaging things students do. Keeping in mind the correlation between frequency of assessment and pops in achievement, teachers should implement strategies that promote this ongoing process throughout the lesson, not just at the end of the learning session.

The strategies that follow provide readily apparent evidence of student progress. Further, they free teachers from the desk-to-desk or front-of-the-room model so that they can distribute content expertise more efficiently. Conversations are natural, safe, and goal-oriented. These strategies bring the strengths of the performance arena into the classroom because they allow teachers to monitor understanding and provide accurate, growth-oriented feedback right this minute—when it matters.

Stick It!

Sticky notes are sheer perfection as a formative assessment tool, enabling teachers to immediately adjust instruction based on real-time individual and class data. It works like this: first, the teacher asks a question to check for students' understanding of the concept being taught. Then students, working individually or in pairs, write down their responses on a sticky note. To keep the focus of the activity purely on ungraded feedback and to ensure confidentiality, the teacher should use only one color of sticky note and request that students write their names on the reverse (sticky) side of the note. When they are ready, students splash their answers on the board (see Figure 4.1). Having students come

FIGURE 4.1
Sticky-Note Assessment

up to the board with their notes whenever they're ready usually gives the teacher a bit of time to examine answers. Still, there will be times when every student seems to rush up at once. When this happens, it can be helpful to sort the notes by common misconceptions.

Once students have posted their notes, the teacher can scan the responses for any misconceptions and provide immediate, descriptive feedback directly tied to the learning goal. This strategy makes common misconceptions evident; in fact, they practically jump out from the board. If there is widespread misunderstanding—say, if 15 students had incorrect responses—the teacher can say, "What great information this is! Let me explain a piece a lot of us are missing in a different way so that we are all clear." After the teacher reteaches the concept, students can adjust their responses and return their sticky notes to the board. After this second round, the teacher again reviews students' responses and provides further feedback. If a handful of students have lingering mis-conceptions, the teacher can pair them with students who have demon-strated understanding or confer with just these few before they continue with their work.

Although this strategy works for all students, it is ideal for struggling students. First, the novelty of the activity makes it immediately engaging, and the small size of the sticky note makes the task seem doable, not overwhelming. Of equal importance is the safety element: if a student makes an error, it's not public. Plus, students get another opportunity to get it right. With just a little help, students can return to the board with the right answer, which feels great!

Sticky notes can be used in a multitude of ways to assess students' attainment of the learning objective. For example, you could have stu-dents use sticky notes to

- Create a Venn diagram comparing command and market economies.
- Compare and contrast two characters from a story.
- Explain the difference between a metaphor and a simile and give an example of each.
- Calculate the area of a circle.
- Draw pictures of a solid, a liquid, and a gas.

Teachers can use these at the end of class as the "Stick-Its Out the Door" strategy—a final formative assessment opportunity for the day that presents one last chance to gauge students' progress toward the learning goal. Sometimes, the end-of-class rush leaves us holding a stack of assessments, watching students race away down the hall and calling, "Wait, come back! You misunderstood this!" Stick-Its Out the Door is a more manageable way to administer a final check for understanding. For added novelty, students can stick their notes around the door. Keep in mind that although the activity itself provides some practice, its real value lies in the feedback and changes to instruction that result. As the last check for the day, errors should be less frequent, but teachers can use the concrete data they garner to differentiate instruction as needed the next day.

Sticky notes can also be used on a larger scale. For example, a school could assign each department a day of the week to collect sticky-note data on students' understanding of the day's learning goal. For example, English language arts teachers could collect data on Mondays, math teachers on Tuesdays, and so on. Then each department or grade level could collaboratively analyze these assessments to see the big picture of student progress. After examining the data, teachers could discuss the questions "What percentage of our students got it today? And what will we do differently tomorrow?"

Cubes

Similar to dice but containing lesson topics instead of numbers on their sides, cubes are a wonderfully engaging, kinesthetic vehicle for promoting rich academic conversations among students. (Although you can find cube templates online, I purchase foldable two-inch-square jewelry boxes at the crafts store or online and then attach a sticky note containing a topic to each side, removing and reusing the topics as needed.) In groups of two, three, or four, students take turns rolling a cube or cubes. Whichever side comes up is the topic the group must discuss. As students roll the cubes and discuss their learning, and as teachers observe students' learning and respond appropriately, all three tiers of feedback naturally emerge: self, peer, and teacher. Because students are still learning and processing the information, they may need to use class notes or other resources to scaffold the process.

The cube strategy is highly versatile: it can be used in every subject area and grade level (for younger students, cubes may contain only pictures) and is easily differentiated. For example, in an English class, some groups may roll a single cube containing examples of literary devices (e.g., *metaphor, simile,* and *personification*) and be tasked with defining and giving an example of whichever term is rolled. Other groups may roll an additional cube containing common words like *clock, water,* and *pepper.* These students, who have already shown an understanding of the literary devices, must use the literary device in a way that incorporates the common word. For example, a student who rolls *personification* and *clock* may say, "The alarm clock moaned at 5:00 a.m." The next student may roll *alliteration* and *water* and say, "Water is wonderfully wet."

Cubes can be incorporated into practically any lesson. Teachers can easily transform a dry textbook activity into hands-on learning using cubes. Figure 4.2 shows some ideas to spark your imagination.

Bow Ties

The bow tie is a versatile tool I created that always receives positive feedback from teachers and students. A mechanism for practice, reading, and peer feedback, it is also ideal for higher-order thinking tasks, such as compare and contrast or listing pros and cons of a topic, and for math practice. As a bonus, it has the ability to make a class of 30 students feel like one of 15.

Here's how it works. Working in pairs, students situate their desks so they are facing each other. On chart paper, each pair draws the outline

FIGURE 4.2
Examples of Cube Topics

Science	Social Studies	English Language Arts	Math
• Respiratory system • Weather • Animal classifications • Cell parts • Planets	• Presidents • Geography terms • Eras • Government branches • Economic systems	• Story elements • Parts of speech • Parts of essays • Genres • Points of view	• Inequalities • Fractions • Types of numbers • Integers • Plotting points

of a bow tie. Then the teacher assigns the task, aligned with the day's learning goal. Each pair divides up the task, with each student first working alone on his or her side of the bow tie. For example, if the task is to compare and contrast series and parallel circuits, each student examines and records information on one type of circuit. Next, the partners share their work and combine their knowledge and findings in the center of the tie. For this task, they might construct a diagram of the two circuits with brief explanations.

Bow ties are an ideal way to differentiate instruction. For a reading task, for example, one student may be assigned a longer passage than her partner, whose passage may be leveled or include more pictures or graphs to scaffold the text. If a passage contains difficult vocabulary, some students might benefit from the inclusion of synonyms of those words.

A bow tie has an additional purpose in math: practice. Students are assigned several problems, which they first work on individually. After this practice, partners confer about their work—"How did you get the answer to the second problem?"—and reach consensus on their answers, teaching each other along the way. In the center of the bow tie, students write their consensus answers. Figure 4.3 shows an example of a math bow tie.

FIGURE 4.3
Math Bow Tie

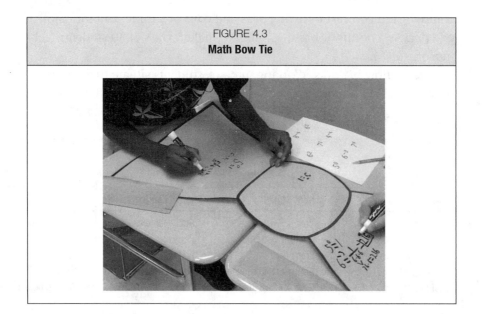

The bow tie strategy enables teachers to move into a facilitative, feedback-giving role and rove around the room as needed. Standing just about anywhere, teachers can easily hear students' conversations and see their thinking evolve. After working in a bow tie format, students are likely to be better prepared to advance to independent work.

Sorts

Sorts are an example of how assessments used for formative purposes can perform multiple roles. Sorts make compelling openers and are useful for practicing vocabulary, and at the same time, they can work as a formative assessment tool. The beauty of sorts is that they are so much fun to do, students don't even realize they are being assessed!

Sorts are endlessly versatile: perfect for pairs and small groups, they can also be completed individually. Teachers can structure sorts as agree/disagree, true/false, categorization, or sequencing exercises. Students can sort ancient peoples, religions, types of food, or types of numbers. Worms, clouds, parts of the body: practically anything that can be studied can be sorted. Sorts can even contain all pictures, such as angles or shapes. It can be helpful to provide an answer key in a folder for student self-assessment. When students get stuck, they can take a sneak peek to advance their progress.

The sort shown in Figure 4.4 (p. 70), created by 6th grade science teachers Ms. Freeman and Ms. Lewis, serves two roles: as a formative assessment tool and as a strategy to deepen vocabulary understanding during a lesson on heat transfer. Students were asked to sort images and facts into categories like *greenhouse effect, radiation, convection,* and *conduction.*

Student Whiteboards

Personal student whiteboards have been a fixture in math classrooms for a while, but they present benefits for other classes as well. It is easier for teachers to see (and therefore respond to) answers on whiteboards than it is to look at answers written in notebooks. Students like whiteboards, too: it's always more fun to write on a board than on paper, and the small size of the boards makes tasks seem manageable.

The magic of formative assessment more often lies in the feedback than in the assessment itself, and whiteboards make giving that

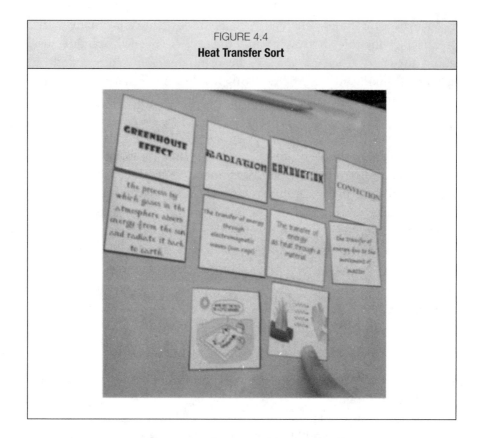

FIGURE 4.4
Heat Transfer Sort

feedback much easier. As students hold up their work, the teacher is able to scan the whole class's responses and give descriptive, timely feedback aimed at moving students toward attainment of the learning goal. Struggling students do not respond well to binary "right, wrong, right, wrong" feedback, but they *do* respond to goals and a clear learning process (Sousa, 2008).

Whiteboards are versatile tools: students can work on them individually or in pairs to create Venn diagrams and flowcharts, write short responses to questions, draw pictures, explain vocabulary words, delineate the pros and cons of an argument, or create metaphors. Best of all, whiteboards can be used daily to yield important data and provide targeted, effective feedback.

Carousels

Named for the round-the-room thinking process it entails, *carouseling* (sometimes referred to as a *gallery walk*) is a highly engaging, kinesthetic instructional strategy that has students collaborate on responses to questions or prompts.

First, the teacher tapes chart paper on the wall at various points in the room. After strategically grouping students and having each group choose a team leader, the teacher assigns a different-colored marker to each group. This step enables each group's answers to be clearly discerned. Then the teacher writes a different question or topic on each piece of chart paper, and groups rotate through all the stations. The leader's job is to listen to group members' responses and develop a common, concise answer for the group.

The questions or topics should be open-ended enough to allow for a variety of responses. For example, if a social studies class has been studying the 1970s, topics might include world conflicts, culture, politics, race relations, and a comparison to another decade. In language arts, the teacher may write a different vocabulary word on each paper and ask groups to create a different metaphor for each word. In math, the teacher could write four problems on each paper and have groups rotate through the stations in two rounds, solving the first two problems during the first round and solving the last two problems on the second round. After the carousel is complete, groups return to their home stations to review all the work on their home paper, correcting responses as needed.

In any subject area, carousels yield useful feedback based on data that emerge during the activity and when students share out their findings at the end. Students naturally tend to provide spot-on feedback to their teammates, and if there is a miscue, it is readily apparent and the teacher can quickly intervene as the content expert.

Communication Devices

Students who are not doing well in school tend to be reluctant to make their academic status public. Rather than chime in with an incorrect response and risk embarrassment, they refrain from participating or seeking assistance. As Jensen (2005) explains, their brains focus more on avoiding danger than on learning.

For teachers, this poses a challenge: to provide effective instruction, we need to know how our students are doing. In essence, we must get students to *communicate* with us—a task that can be easier said than done. Asking the generic "Everybody got it?" reaps only nods. And many commonly used checks for understanding, while novel and fun, do not provide the immediate, accurate data we are seeking. For example, asking students for a thumbs-up or thumbs-down depending on whether or not they understand the concept can be problematic: not only do students prefer not to advertise the fact that they're lost, but the position of a thumb also fails to provide adequate information for assessing students' status on the learning goal. Using traffic indicators, such as red and green cups, poses a similar problem: placing a bright-red cup on their desks all too clearly signals students' current state of academic affairs. It's fine to use novel forms of formative assessment, but if we want to get and give useful feedback and calibrate our instruction accordingly, our methods must prompt students to show, specifically, what they know. Two communication devices that elicit honest, fruitful responses from all students, in my experience, are *sticky bar graphs* and *peaks and valleys*.

Sticky bar graphs. Sticky bar graphs enable the teacher to quickly gauge how the class is doing as a whole. If students had six homework questions the previous night, for example, the teacher can write the numbers 1–6 on a piece of chart paper, provide each student with a sticky dot, and ask, "If we had time to discuss just one homework question, which one would you like it to be?" Students then place their dots above the number of the question that posed the biggest challenge for them. With a quick glance, the teacher can ascertain the areas that need the most clarification.

Teachers can use this tool for a larger lesson review or test preparation, too. For example, a teacher who wants to get students ready for a test on the parts of cells can write down the parts on a piece of chart paper and, again, have students place one or two dots on the area or areas where they still have confusion. The example in Figure 4.5 shows a sticky bar graph from an English class about to review the parts of

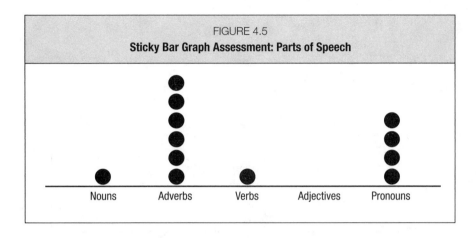

FIGURE 4.5
Sticky Bar Graph Assessment: Parts of Speech

Nouns   Adverbs   Verbs   Adjectives   Pronouns

speech. Clearly, students would like more practice on adverbs and pronouns (but have a strong grasp of adjectives).

This strategy is meant to be a quick check; obviously, a dot does not provide specific feedback. However, the strategy gives students a safe way to communicate where they need help. In fact, you may see visible signs of relief as students realize that their classmates are experiencing similar challenges.

Peaks and valleys. A peak and valley is a graph on which students identify their strengths and weaknesses. Teachers can have students assess their knowledge, on a scale of 1 to 100, of anything from types of parasites to the branches of government. In the example shown in Figure 4.6 (p. 74), the student has evaluated her knowledge of cumulus clouds as high but needs further instruction on altostratus clouds.

Teachers can also use peaks and valleys for pre-assessment purposes. For example, before beginning a unit on fractions, a math teacher could have students use a colored marker to create a peak and valley showing their current level of knowledge of addition, subtraction, division, and multiplication of fractions. Later in the unit, before the class begins reviewing material for the summative exam, students can use a different color on the same peak and valley to indicate their latest level of expertise. Although they will still have some weak areas, they are also likely to have grown considerably. Having students use the peaks and valleys

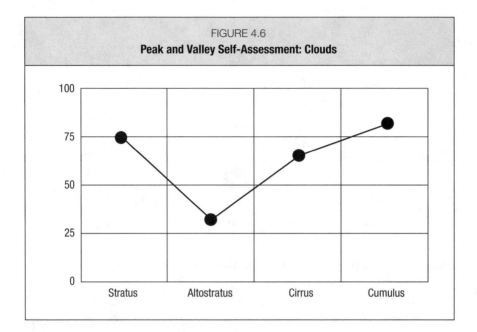

FIGURE 4.6

Peak and Valley Self-Assessment: Clouds

strategy has academic and motivational benefits: it is both informative and empowering for students to be able to track their own progress.

Reflections on Formative Assessment and Feedback

It is essential for all our students—but particularly low-achieving students—that we make thoughtful classroom assessment decisions. We know that to help students, we need to be able to see what they know. Yet some have become masters at concealing their struggles.

The assessments discussed in this chapter are safe and ungraded but make learning highly visible. Rather than relying on just one person in the room to provide guidance, they involve all learners in the feedback process. Perhaps most important, they enable instruction to pivot *right now* to help students, not days later. As a side benefit, they don't look like assessments at all; rolling a cube and putting sorts together feel more like games.

Each opportunity to provide feedback based on formative assessment brings another opportunity for students to learn—to get better at a task. In addition, a steady stream of descriptive feedback based on minute-by-minute assessments can help students gather academic steam and confidence for high-stakes scored assessments. These multiple opportunities to revise and improve work can foster new optimism and effort in struggling learners, who begin to see the benefit to fixing errors, revising writing, or rereading a passage.

Armed with the knowledge of the potential achievement gains that formative assessment and subsequent feedback can produce may mean changing some old classroom habits. Students tentatively positioning their thumbs in the air will not yield the information required to make precise instructional adjustments. Rather than asking, "Any questions?" it's time to start saying, "Everybody grab a sticky note!"

Checklist for formative assessment and feedback:

- ❑ Assessments are explicitly linked to the learning goal.
- ❑ Assessments are multiple and distributed throughout the learning session.
- ❑ Feedback is timely.
- ❑ Feedback explicitly focuses on student attainment of the learning goal.
- ❑ Feedback opportunities are tiered and include the teacher, students themselves, and their peers.
- ❑ Throughout the learning session, instructional decisions are based on observable evidence of student learning.

5

Vocabulary Development:
Implementing a Strategic Plan

Sharpened number 2 pencils in hand, nervous students settle into their desks for a high-stakes standardized test. For many, just understanding the questions will be problematic, especially if they lack understanding of content-area vocabulary. Students will encounter even more difficulty if they have gaps in their incidental vocabulary, which includes all those words they really should know by now.

Here is an excerpt from a 7th grade math question that might be found on a standardized test:

> Which of the following equations depicts the situation if *T* represents the number of times he can play during the summer?

To correctly respond to this question, students would need to possess a solid working knowledge of the math word *equations*. In addition, it would be helpful if they could retrieve the words *depicts, situation,* and *represents* from their incidental vocabulary. A student weak in vocabulary, however, may opt to give up on this question and move on to the next.

In the social studies portion of the test, students are called upon to interpret primary sources, such as the following passage from the Declaration of Independence:

> Prudence, indeed, will dictate that Governments long established
> should not be changed for light and transient causes; and accordingly
> all experience hath shewn, that mankind are more disposed to suffer,

while evils are sufferable, than to right themselves by abolishing the forms to which they are accustomed.

The vocabulary is daunting right from the start, with the word *prudence*. To interpret and respond to this sentence, students would also need to understand the words *transient, dictate, establish,* and *abolish,* as well as infer the meaning of archaic words like *hath* and *shewn*. An inadequate vocabulary could render a student unable to understand arguably the most important document in U.S. history.

Science has its own unique vocabulary. In the following question, all of the responses contain academic vocabulary, a common element on standardized tests:

Which of these is *not* a characteristic of an arthropod? (A) Exoskeleton (B) Jointed appendages (C) Hydrostatic skeleton (D) Internal cavities

In a brief moment of a stressful testing situation, students must recall with clarity the meanings of biology terms like *exoskeleton, hydrostatic skeleton,* and *appendages*. In addition, they must be able to retrieve words such as *jointed, internal,* and *cavities* from their bank of incidental word knowledge.

This vocabulary barrier doesn't hinder students just on standardized tests. Class conversations, teachers' lectures, the texts students read, and the online resources they use all contain academic and incidental vocabulary. To express themselves during a science lab, work collaboratively in language arts, or ask for detailed help in math, students must know specific vocabulary. To master content the first time they learn it, students must understand the language of the content.

An inadequate vocabulary can make it difficult for students to demonstrate subject proficiency and may even be academically debilitating. In large measure, to be successful in school, students must know the right words.

The Daunting (and Somewhat Depressing) Reality of Vocabulary Development

Vocabulary touches every aspect of students' development as academically literate learners, strongly influencing their reading, writing, and conversational proficiencies. Everything, it seems, is harder for students when they lack an adequate vocabulary. Coming to grips with the frustrating nature of vocabulary gaps begins with understanding first why many students do not know the words they should already know and, second, why learners have difficulty retaining and recalling new vocabulary. The following sections discuss three major challenges affecting vocabulary development.

Vocabulary Challenge 1: Many Students Arrive with Vocabulary Gaps

Many students begin their academic careers with significant gaps in their vocabularies, not knowing many of the words that their peers have already learned at home. This vocabulary divide falls largely along socioeconomic lines. What is particularly disheartening is the young age at which the vocabulary divide begins: Hart and Risley (1995) established the correlation between family income and vocabulary gaps in children as young as 3 years old. They found that 3-year-olds from welfare families typically possess just 70 percent of the vocabulary of children living in working-class homes. The gap widens when we look at children of middle-class, professional parents: children from families on welfare possessed just 45 percent of the vocabulary of the more affluent children. The researchers found that when talking to their 1- and 2-year-olds, professional parents use a richer variety of words and tenses, ask more questions, and provide more positive feedback than do their low-socioeconomic-status (SES) counterparts.

Students with vocabulary gaps pay a steep price for the words they do not know. Becker (1977) drew a strong connection between poor vocabulary and academic failure in his evaluation of reading and language programs for disadvantaged students. As tests began including more adult-like vocabulary—typically by the end of 3rd grade—the failure rate rose.

Unfortunately, according to Nagy and Herman (1984), vocabulary gaps extend well into the upper grades. Standardized tests show a significant divide between high and low achievers: students in grades 4–12 who score at the 50th percentile know 6,000 more words than do students scoring at the 25th percentile. As students who arrive at school with larger, more varied vocabularies continue to grow their vocabularies, learners from disadvantaged homes that are less likely to support vocabulary growth are more likely to fall behind in school—and the gap continues to widen.

Low-achieving students' vocabulary gaps may stymie efforts to move them out of the bottom of the academic pack. These gaps may have begun long before their current teachers met them, but these holes in understanding can make it more difficult for them to master new concepts, comprehend a passage, or succeed on tests.

Vocabulary Challenge 2: Students Face a Barrage of New Academic Vocabulary

Vocabulary development is not static, but fast-moving and ongoing. Teachers in every subject area tack on more words every day. A social studies teacher might introduce 20 new words this week, the science teacher 12, the language arts teacher 10, and the math teacher 7. Students with weak vocabularies now face a barrage of new, unfamiliar words. The question becomes, *are students gaining ground on vocabulary or adding to their existing gaps?*

Figure 5.1 (p. 80), adapted from a table in *Building Background Knowledge for Academic Achievement* (Marzano, 2004), shows the number of new vocabulary words students are exposed to by grade bands. The number of new words students are expected to learn and retain is simply staggering.

The volume of vocabulary being introduced in grades 3–5 may seem surprising, being on par with the number of new words introduced to high school students. This may support Becker's (1977) premise that the increase in adult-like vocabulary being introduced late in 3rd grade contributes to failure among students with vocabulary gaps.

Vocabulary Challenge 3: Reading Is Not Enough to Build Vocabulary

In their research with 5th graders, Jenkins and colleagues (1984) found that it was not easy for students to learn new vocabulary on their own and advised educators that prescribing large amounts of reading will not effectively build students' vocabularies. Why? Largely because students need multiple exposures—typically, six—to new words to be able to grasp, retain, and use them.

FIGURE 5.1
Number of Terms per Level by Subject Area

Subject	Level 1 K–2	Level 2 3–5	Level 3 6–8	Level 4 9–12	Total
Mathematics	80	190	201	214	685
Science	100	166	225	282	773
Social studies (history, civics, economics, and geography)	325	1,384	1,300	1,383	4,392
English language arts	83	245	247	223	798
Health	60	68	75	77	280
Physical education	57	100	50	34	241
Arts (art, dance, music, theater, and visual arts)	54	198	198	99	549
Technology	23	47	56	79	205
Totals	782	2,398	2,352	2,391	7,923

Source: From *Building Background Knowledge for Academic Achievement* (p. 115), by R. J. Marzano, 2004, Alexandria, VA: ASCD. Copyright 2004 by ASCD.

This is not to say that students don't learn any new words while reading, but it is more difficult than we might realize. Swanborn and de Glopper's (1999) meta-analysis showed that in the course of normal reading, high-achieving students tended to learn only about 19 percent of the unknown words they encountered, while middle achievers learned about 12 percent and low-achieving students learned only 8 percent. Although reading is certainly one component in developing a strong vocabulary, low-achieving students in particular are not likely to learn many unfamiliar words during their reading. First, as Beck, McKeown, and Kucan (2002) point out, these students are typically less proficient than their higher-achieving peers are at using context clues to understand new words. In addition, they are less likely to be reading texts containing large numbers of unfamiliar words.

Just as reading alone doesn't necessarily help develop vocabulary, possessing a poor vocabulary has severe implications for reading and learning. Research (Vacca & Vacca, 2002) confirms what many educators witness in the classroom: there is a strong correlation between vocabulary knowledge and reading comprehension. When learners are unfamiliar with the words they encounter in print, they have trouble understanding any of what they have read. Many struggling students don't know enough of the right words to understand the text to begin with. In general, poor readers read less than good readers do, and when they do, the text is typically less rigorous. The tragic cycle that Stanovich (1986) refers to as the *Matthew effect* often ensues: the weak readers get weaker while the strong readers get stronger.

The Trouble with Context Clues and Dictionaries

Exacerbating the vocabulary challenges faced by both students and teachers is the fact that many common practices for vocabulary development simply don't work.

We've already seen that reading, in isolation, fails to build students' vocabularies adequately. Unfortunately, this continues to be a popularly used practice. In class, teachers will sometimes tell students to "get the meaning from the context." The chances of a student piecing together a word's meaning from the surrounding text depend both on the individual student's ability and on the text itself. For example, when students are grappling with dense text that contains a large number of unfamiliar words, the odds are remote that they will be able to use context clues to discern meaning. In fact, students have just a 7 percent chance of understanding new words from that kind of dense text (Swanborn & de Glopper, 1999). I jokingly tell teachers that we don't want the chances of our students learning new words to be in the same range as their odds of getting struck by lightning.

Another traditional approach that is largely ineffective is having students look up unfamiliar words in glossaries or dictionaries. Students usually do not understand these formal definitions and benefit more from reading or hearing explanations phrased in everyday language. The language in dictionary definitions can be vague and contain multiple interpretations of words that can get students off course (Beck et al., 2002). In addition, students who rely on dictionary definitions tend to have difficulty using the words in context; instead of actually *learning* the words, they just memorize definitions. As a result, when teachers discuss these words in terms that differ from the dictionary definitions, they often get a sea of blank faces.

Why Strategic Vocabulary Development Works

The significant vocabulary challenges faced by struggling students, as well as the ineffectiveness of certain vocabulary instruction strategies, might dampen some teachers' enthusiasm for teaching vocabulary. But there is good news! First, best practices in vocabulary instruction can yield significant gains in academic achievement. Second, vocabulary strategies have the potential to be the most engaging part of class: if we play our cards right, students will actually look forward to learning vocabulary.

We know that vocabulary knowledge strongly correlates to reading proficiency and academic achievement. Stahl and Fairbanks (1986) found that learners at the 50th percentile who received direct instruction in the words they would encounter scored, on average, as well in reading comprehension as did students at the 83rd percentile.

In addition, in their review of studies examining the role of academic vocabulary proficiency in student success, Nagy and Townsend (2012) report that all students who received direct vocabulary instruction, including English language learners, outperformed students who did not. This vocabulary instruction incorporated strategies like graphic organizers, discussions, and paired collaborations.

The research reveals what educators know instinctively: students need to know the right words to gain a deep understanding of content. As Marzano (2004) puts it, "Simply stated, direct instruction in vocabulary works" (p. 68).

Implementing a Strategic Vocabulary Plan

There are some fundamental principles of vocabulary instruction that powerfully affect the development of students' vocabularies. These are vital to keep in mind as you create and implement a plan for strategic vocabulary instruction.

Principle 1: Multiple exposures are necessary to build true mastery. Vocabulary instruction is not a one-shot deal (Beck et al., 2002; Jenkins et al., 1984; Nagy & Townsend, 2012; Stahl & Fairbanks, 1986). A strategic vocabulary plan purposefully weaves multiple experiences with words throughout a unit. Academic vocabulary development is a journey that deepens students' understanding of words over the course of a unit, and students benefit from getting numerous, varied opportunities to use new words.

Principle 2: The V in *vocabulary* is for *visual*. Nonlinguistic representations of words enhance students' understanding. Powell (1980) found that students whose vocabulary instruction incorporated nonlinguistic representations scored 37 percent higher than students who relied solely on looking up definitions and 21 percent higher than students whose practice consisted of generating sentences using new vocabulary. Integrating nontext experiences in a strategic vocabulary plan—for example, having students draw pictures of new words, act them out, or trace angles on walls—deepens comprehension and learning.

Principle 3: High-impact vocabulary instruction engages learners in interactions with words. Learners gain a deeper understanding of vocabulary with interactive strategies involving discussions, games, comparisons, classifications, and associations (Beck et al., 2002; Marzano, 2004; Vacca & Vacca, 2002). Vocabulary instruction can be the most engaging, hands-on component of any lesson.

Principle 4: Effective instruction focuses on words students need to know now. If we want students to internalize and "own" academic vocabulary, they need to practice words in context. The goal is to support students' learning by developing the vocabulary they need to understand the content being taught right now (Nagy & Townsend, 2012). Teachers should first identify critical academic vocabulary and then develop a deliberate plan that deepens students' understanding of those words.

Principle 5: Incidental vocabulary is important, too. Rather than focusing exclusively on academic vocabulary, teachers should continue developing students' incidental vocabulary by modeling the use of non-content-area words that students need to know. It is important to encourage students to engage in discussion and wide reading and to continue reading to students throughout their school careers. Students benefit from teachers who share their rich vocabulary.

Graves (2006) emphasizes the importance of building primary-level students' incidental vocabularies through rich listening and discussion activities, particularly because the books students read at this level often do not contain much new vocabulary. In the upper grades, Graves recommends, teachers should continue building students' incidental vocabularies by deliberately using more challenging words in classroom discussions.

Strategies to Develop Strong Vocabularies

Helping students build their academic vocabularies is like going on a journey that moves students from darkness to light. Before their first exposure to new words, students are in the dark. With each subsequent, meaningful exposure, however, the light gets brighter. By the time they have made multiple connections by comparing, drawing, sorting, and discussing the words, the light has reached its full brightness: we have helped students move from zero knowledge to surface-level knowledge to deep, lasting understanding.

During this journey, we add new words gradually, not all at once. The first step in planning meaningful, systematic vocabulary instruction is to decide which words are most instrumental to students' attainment of the content. There are seemingly a million words students don't know, but which ones matter most right now? Which ones are most likely to create a barrier to understanding? Creating a list of those words is a crucial early step in mapping out a vocabulary plan for the unit. This list is for teachers' planning purposes, not for students; the words will be unveiled to students over time. The list should encompass just vocabulary words, not historical or literary figures or important events. Remember: because students require multiple exposures to gain deep understanding of words, the list must be strategic and manageable.

Another consideration to keep in mind when developing a unit's vocabulary plan is which strategies work best at the beginning, the middle, and the end of lessons or units. The key factor determining when to implement each strategy is the prior knowledge required. For each strategy that follows, I explain the optimal time for implementation.

TIP Charts

As we discussed in Chapter 2, a TIP is an anchor chart that scaffolds vocabulary learning. The TIP makes announcing a new word a big deal: the teacher introduces the word with fanfare, has the students say it, provides a student-friendly definition, and creates a nonverbal representation. The TIP acknowledges to students that deepening one's vocabulary is a process, not a one-time deal. Although adding a word to the TIP usually occurs when students first encounter the term, the TIP remains for the duration of the unit. As students proceed through the unit, they continually use the TIP as a reference guide. The TIP can also reappear later in the year for standardized test review.

Classrooms that use TIPs look and sound different from those that don't. In one classroom I visited recently, a teacher used an academic vocabulary word that was unfamiliar to students. As if on cue, students' heads turned toward the TIP for reference. The word was not there. The teacher laughed and said, "Oh, my gosh! We forgot to put that on our TIP, didn't we?"

It is also helpful to have students maintain TIP charts in their notebooks for personal reference. The TIP in Ms. Bracewell's middle school math class, pictured in Figure 5.2 (p. 86), matches the format that students use in their notebooks. Definitions and illustrations are student-friendly and collaboratively produced.

Secondary teachers who teach multiple courses would create a TIP for each course. (Note that they are not expected to create a new TIP for each section of a single course.) They can use sticky arrows or other tools to demonstrate that a new word has been added to the TIP when appropriate for each class. Some teachers conceal new words with paper and unveil them each period with a dramatic flourish.

Word Art

Word art is a strategy that students truly enjoy. Creative and engaging, it accords with research supporting the use of nonlinguistic representations in vocabulary development. Although I sometimes need to remind the more painstaking students that this is not a "Monet moment" but a "stick-figure moment," this strategy does give artistic students a chance to shine.

FIGURE 5.2
Math TIP Chart

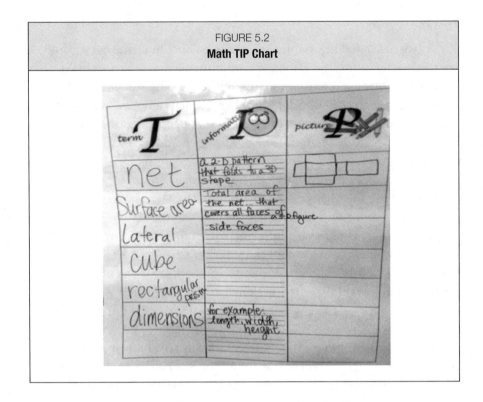

The goal of word art is to make a word's meaning clear by making art out of the actual text of the word. For example, the word *parallel* could be written multiple times, with each instance of the word parallel to the last. The word *circumference* could scroll around a circle. *Latitude* could be scrawled across a drawing of a globe. These are examples of concrete terms, but abstract concepts like *popular sovereignty* or *radiation* work wonderfully as well.

Figure 5.3 shows how the term *arable* inspired one student to sketch a cornstalk to stand for the *L* and how another student separated each syllable of *segregation* to illustrate the word's meaning.

Word art provides students with a moment to think about a new term and feel inspired to create something original. It is a particularly useful strategy when the teacher has introduced and is using a new word during class. Thus, this strategy is normally used early in a lesson, but it can also be used at learning stations and during reviews.

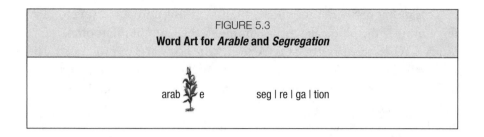

FIGURE 5.3
Word Art for *Arable* and *Segregation*

arab e   seg | re | ga | tion

Quirky Comparisons

The quirky comparisons strategy is a fun way to explore words, and it allows multiple correct responses, so students can feel safe participating. To use this strategy, teachers first cut random pictures out of magazines and place them in a bag. The bag may contain, for example, pictures of lipstick, a zebra, a roller coaster, and peanut butter—pretty much anything goes as long as it is recognizable to students! Working in pairs or small groups, students reach into their bag and randomly select a picture or two. Then they must complete a sentence provided by the teacher (e.g., "A _____ is like _____ because _____.") that incorporates a word drawn from the bag and one or two key words that have been added to the TIP that day. To complete the sentence, students must brainstorm analogies between the two terms. For example, if the new vocabulary word is *depression*, students might come up with the sentence "Peanut butter is like a depression because that's about all families could afford during a bad economy" or "A roller coaster is like a depression because not having a job can make a breadwinner feel nauseated . . . just like a roller coaster does."

Teachers can use this strategy at different points throughout a lesson, but not during students' first encounter with a word. Students need a little background knowledge to be successful.

Action!

This strategy is perfect for the middle of a unit, when students need practice with a handful of words. First, the teacher places students in pairs. One student plays the role of a movie director while the other plays an actor. The director draws a word from the bag (the same type as the one used for the quirky comparisons strategy) and shares it with just his or her partner. After quietly brainstorming and rehearsing for a few minutes, the pairs take turns coming to the front of the room—the "stage." When the director calls "Action!" the actor acts out the word. The actor may not speak or use words to portray the term, but for added fun, teachers may consider allowing props. After each pair acts out its word, the rest of the class must guess the word. One rule: the word must be acted out in the correct context. For example, if students draw the word *cell* in science class, they cannot act out a cell phone.

Teachers can easily differentiate this activity by strategically grouping students who have greater knowledge of the vocabulary with students who have more emergent vocabularies. Acting out new vocabulary not only is fun, collaborative, and engaging but also deeply reinforces academic vocabulary through multiple exposures.

Which One Doesn't Belong?

Toward the middle and end of a unit, students have been introduced to many words, and their prior knowledge has deepened owing to daily, multiple exposures. "Which One Doesn't Belong?" is a thinking strategy that teachers can use around this time to review and reinforce new vocabulary. The teacher simply provides a list of vocabulary words, either by projecting it onto a screen or by cutting it into pieces of paper for a more kinesthetic approach, and students must decide which word they think doesn't belong with the others. For this activity, pairs work well. Teachers should keep in mind that it is more effective to create a list that has multiple correct answers. The point is not for students to get the "right" answer but to foster critical thinking and analysis and encourage students to provide reasoning for their choices. For example, look at the following list provided during a social studies unit on the American Revolution.

Which One Doesn't Belong . . . and Why?

Militia	Patriot
Colonist	Navy SEAL
Army	Defense
Soldier	Infantry

One potential answer is *colonist*, because the rest of the words have something to do with the military. Another student might suggest *Navy SEAL*, because it does not belong in the time period. Throughout this thought-provoking activity, students hear a variety of justifications and points of view, which further deepens their understanding of the words.

Instant Etch A Sketch

This strategy, which combines vocabulary development with hands-on fun, works for any grade level. The teacher divides students into pairs and then pours salt on plates or cookie sheets and provides each student with a cotton swab to use as a stylus. Then the teacher gives a vocabulary task, such as "Draw an acute angle. Have your partner check it." After partners complete this task, they gently shake the plate to erase the answer in preparation for the next task: "Look at the angle on the board. Write down the name of that angle." And so on. Teachers can use this activity to have students practice spelling, create Venn diagrams, illustrate vocabulary words, and even review content for standardized tests. This strategy, which doubles as formative assessment, fits beautifully from the middle of a lesson to test review.

The novelty of working in salt makes this strategy quite engaging, especially for kinesthetic and visual learners, and having students collaborate with partners creates an environment in which students share information with one another.

Word Detective

In this simple but effective activity, the teacher hands out a lesson-related passage that is missing critical vocabulary words. The best time to use this strategy is typically the middle or toward the end of the lesson, depending on the number of words selected. Working in pairs, students discuss context clues and determine which words belong in the blanks. Here is a sample word detective text:

> Some abolitionists worked in secret to help _____ escape to freedom. They set up a system known as the _____ Railroad. The Underground _____ was a series of escape _____ and hiding places

to bring slaves out of the _____. The most famous _____ on the railroad was Harriet Tubman. She helped about 300 people escape to the _____ and became a symbol of the _____ movement.

Many times, more than one word will fit in a blank, which is fine. As with "Which One Doesn't Belong?" this strategy aims not to get all students to come up with the same correct answer, but to cultivate thinking and reasoning skills and reading comprehension and encourage sharing of knowledge.

Vocabulary Cubes

Cubes, discussed in Chapter 4 as a formative assessment strategy, also make wonderful vocabulary development tools. First, the teacher writes down a different vocabulary word on each of the six sides of one cube. On the second cube, the teacher writes different directions on each side, such as *draw, explain, provide a synonym, give a nonexample, say as a group four times,* and *explain what it means using an Italian accent.* Students roll the cubes and follow the directions for their vocabulary word. Cubes are also great as station activities. A teacher can use this strategy more than once during a lesson, and add a second cube deeper into the unit that contains additional terms. This activity is engaging, collaborative, and perfect for kinesthetic learners, and it promotes transfer of learning.

Vocabulary Sorts

Every subject involves some kind of classification, so vocabulary sorts work beautifully in any class. Although they require a bit of work at the front end, sorts are as effective as they are engaging. To save time and maximize effectiveness, teachers should avoid making too many pieces for a single sort, which can cause tedium.

Figure 5.4 shows a fraction sort that a math teacher could use at the beginning of a unit as a pre-assessment, throughout the unit at learning stations, or toward the end of the unit for review. The teacher would simply need to print out and cut up the chart and then place the pieces in small plastic bags. This is an example of a closed sort, which means that the category headings are supplied. Some students benefit from that

			FIGURE 5.4 **Fraction Sort (Unsorted)**			
Equivalent	**Denominator**	**Numerator**	**Mixed number**	**Simplify**	**Improper**	**Proper**
7/21	3/4	17 2/3	2/3	4/8 = 1/2	29/7	4/16 = 1/4
23/209	88/11	7/11	1/4 = 25/100	19/20	4/8 = 16/32 = 50/100	4 1/8

For this sort, the category headings are provided. Some students may receive the sort without headings.

additional support, whereas others will be able to sort the pieces correctly and create the headings on their own. When I create a sort, I typically code the bags with colored sticky dots for easy differentiation—for example, a yellow dot on bags that don't include any category headings, a red dot on bags that include some headings as cues, and a blue dot on bags that include all the headings.

Sorts—even vocabulary sorts—do not need to contain words. Students can classify sorts entirely composed of pictures, showing, for example, types of energy, varying angles, or distinguishing features of cultures and economies. Students can sort by examples and nonexamples, sequence of events, or what belongs and what does not belong. The beauty of sorts is their versatility: students can engage in them many times over the course of a unit, and teachers can revisit sorts after the unit is over as review for standardized tests.

Reflections on Vocabulary Development

From all research has told us about the importance of providing students with direct, strategic instruction in vocabulary, you'd think vocabulary instruction would be a key feature of most classrooms. Unfortunately, the opposite is often true: the practice is actually quite rare in most classrooms (Jenkins et al., 1984). Looking at this situation through a different lens, however, perhaps this is cause for hope: if ever-widening achievement gaps are attributable to inadequate, inconsistent use of best practices, then this problem is potentially fixable!

A strategic vocabulary plan must be deliberately crafted and thoughtfully implemented throughout a unit, acknowledging that vocabulary development is a gradual process. Here's how a vocabulary plan may look in action in a hypothetical classroom: on its first encounter with a word, the class says it aloud and adds it to the TIP, along with a student-friendly definition and a class-generated illustration. Students may construct a word art to reinforce their understanding of the new term. After the teacher adds a second term to the TIP, students compare and contrast the two words. By mid-unit, five terms are on the TIP, and students generate definitions and examples using a carousel approach. Toward the end of the unit, just before the summative assessment, students create sorts to review all seven terms they have learned.

Note how this approach exposes students to new words numerous times and encourages them to engage with the vocabulary in a variety of hands-on ways.

While I was observing a high school class recently, periodic applause kept erupting in the room. Confused, I leaned over and asked a student, "What's all the clapping about?" He said, "When someone uses a vocabulary word correctly, we all clap." This class was making the unit's vocabulary a cause for celebration every day.

And this is as it should be. Knowing the right words empowers students, especially those who are at risk of failing. A deep, broad knowledge of vocabulary is essential to mastering the curriculum the first time. When students walk into a testing session or open a textbook, they need to feel the power of words: "Oh, I know what *surrealism* is!"

As teachers, we sometimes believe our students should know these words because *we* have used them repeatedly throughout the school day or even over the course of years. We may find ourselves asking, "How can you not know what *fulcrum* (or *republic*, or *arachnid*) means? We've been talking about this for three days (or two weeks, or 17 years)!" The fact that we know the words so well actually speaks to the importance of multiple exposures: these words are ingrained in our minds precisely because we have used them authentically and repeatedly. Our challenge is to keep them fresh and exciting as students work with them many times over.

Checklist for vocabulary development:

❑ Students practice and use vocabulary words multiple times in varied ways.

❑ Teachers and students use TIP charts.

❑ Vocabulary instruction integrates visual representations.

❑ Vocabulary is taught in context.

❑ Vocabulary instruction is hands-on and engaging to students.

❑ The vocabulary plan includes the critical words that students need to know.

❑ Incidental vocabulary development is ongoing.

❑ Dictionaries and glossaries are used as tools, not as strategies.

6

Student Work Sessions: Giving Students Greater Responsibility with Valuable Work

Demanding curriculum pacing guides, binders packed with standards, textbooks the size of tires, and the never-ending pressure of scores, scores, scores. The question looms: how can all of this information possibly be packed into students' heads?

The magnitude of this challenge weighs on us. As a result, *we* go home and work, work, work. *We* gather multiple sources. *We* take notes on our reading. *We* synthesize information. *We* separate what's important from what's trivial and divide facts from opinions. *We* infer. *We* visualize. *We* eliminate unreliable sources. *We* create a PowerPoint presentation or a handout with all the information students need on the Industrial Revolution or Shakespeare's sonnets or the circulatory system. *We* draw comparisons, *we* think, and *we* write. . . .

This is why *we* are so frequently on *Jeopardy*. All the work we are doing has made us masters of the content through and through. As we create a flurry of products to deliver to learners, learners are largely taking notes on our thinking. But what are *students* thinking? How would *they* fare on the Daily Double? Where are *their* creations, *their* products, *their* opinions?

This chapter is not about teachers working less or students working more; it's about both sides working differently. It's about content experts choreographing student work sessions in which students do more of the talking, the problem solving, and the creating. During these periods, a significant amount of academic control (and accountability) shifts from our shoulders to theirs.

If we want students to get the content the first time, we must consistently engage them academically. In other words, students need to work hard. That means giving them an important academic job to do. To get low achievers to jump in and contribute at higher levels, we need to thoughtfully structure their work.

The Trouble with Low-Level Work

Low-achieving students might not immediately come to mind during a discussion about increasing critical thinking and collaboration. Struggling learners are more likely to have some missing pieces, including smaller vocabularies, lower reading levels, and gaps in basic skills. Hawkins, Doueck, and Lishner (1988) reported that students who are failing academically also tend to have more discipline issues—a finding plenty of teachers can corroborate. In addition, struggling students may have poor self-esteem and hold low expectations for themselves.

It may seem counterintuitive to place more control of learning in the hands of students who reside in this tenuous academic state. The tendency may be, rather, to assign them more individual seatwork—to give them lower-level work that they can handle. But already-frustrated students and tedium do not mix well.

Unfortunately, it is tedium that students in remediation are often given. Research (Hawkins et al., 1988) suggests that students in lower tracks are the least likely to experience the kinds of instruction most associated with high achievement. According to Shearer, Ruddell, and Vogt (2001), students who are struggling academically tend to get highly structured lessons that offer few opportunities for creativity or interaction with other students. Their higher-achieving classmates, on the other hand, typically experience more interaction, more creative approaches to learning, and more collegial relationships with teachers. These already-successful students also engage more often in higher levels of thinking, independent research, and synthesis. They are even afforded more wait time after questioning.

Echoing those findings, Dicintio and Gee (1999) found a prevalence of low-level skills, routine tasks, and heavy teacher control in classrooms containing demotivated, struggling students. Their study, which focused on students in an alternative setting who had experienced a mixture of discipline and academic problems, found that students became more competent, less bored, and less confused when they were given more control over their learning situations. The researchers concluded that even the most academically and motivationally vulnerable students require challenge and autonomy to thrive.

It is ironic that students who have the greatest need for engaging, compelling instructional strategies often receive the opposite. Not surprisingly, the tendency to provide high-impact instruction to high achievers and less effective instruction to low achievers can exacerbate achievement gaps rather than close them. Still, the reality is that there are barriers to providing struggling students with greater rigor and autonomy. The first barrier to come to many teachers' minds is likely students' low reading levels. Behavior problems and lack of motivation to work hard may follow closely behind. The good news is that the strategies offered in this chapter break down many of these legitimate barriers to learning.

Why Student Work Sessions Work

A student work session follows a thought-provoking opener that sets the stage for new learning and a mini-lesson that explains or models the day's concept. After the mini-lesson, students are ready to work—to process the new information, develop their understanding, and demonstrate their level of mastery. At every step, students' thinking and discussion are visible, and teacher and peer feedback continually improve student work.

Effective student work sessions are characterized by increased student control (and a concomitant increase in personal accountability), high levels of student engagement, visible demonstration of student thinking, and a reliance on cooperative learning.

Cooperative learning is a powerful practice. It cultivates robust interaction among students because team success relies on the contributions of each member of the group. Effective cooperative learning involves much more than just putting students into groups, however. Slavin

(1988) uncovered two essential conditions for effective cooperative learning: individual accountability and an important group goal. Slavin (1983) also indicated that each student's performance must be readily visible and quantifiable to the team. Cooperative learning brings with it a high level of personal accountability: with the team's success on the line, students feel an urgent need to do their best work (Kagan & Kagan, 2009).

Research has established the positive effects of cooperative learning at all education levels, from 1st grade to college, and in every content area. A study (Johnson, Skon, & Johnson, 1980) comparing individual learning with cooperative learning found that in four out of four tasks, students working cooperatively outperformed those working by themselves. The study also found that when students work together toward a common academic goal, they tend to exhibit higher-level problem-solving skills. Potential achievement gains from cooperative learning are impressive: according to Johnson, Maruyama, Johnson, Nelson, and Skon (1981), cooperative learning's effect size is a substantial 0.78. And Marzano and colleagues (2001) identify effective cooperative learning as having a "powerful effect on learning" (p. 87).

A more recent study by Johnson and Johnson (2009) reaffirmed much of the same good news surrounding cooperative learning. Student motivation, it seems, is higher when students work cooperatively rather than individually. This makes sense: when students have a specific job to do and team goals rely on their part of the work, it is natural to feel more motivated. The study also determined that students' self-esteem increases in cooperative settings.

Gillies and Ashman (1998) found that working in groups that have adequate structure reaps added benefits. Learners whose groups have explicit collective and individual goals exhibit more cooperative behaviors, including listening to one another, taking turns, and solving problems together. In addition, students in structured cooperative groups were more helpful, empathetic, and supportive of teammates' endeavors than were students in less-structured groups.

For low-achieving students, structured cooperative learning can be especially helpful. When the group goal relies on each student doing his or her part, groups are less likely to have one or two students doing all of the work and excluding the lower achievers. When grouped with higher-achieving students, struggling learners develop new vocabulary and benefit from higher-level academic conversations that they wouldn't have working alone. Even when a group fails to arrive at a correct answer, lower achievers benefit from observing the thought processes and strategies that higher achievers use to tackle problems.

Although it may seem logical to isolate students who are struggling and give them remedial, passive work, doing just the opposite provides the better remedy. In fact, research (Kagan & Kagan, 2009) indicates that the strongest gains in cooperative learning will likely come from the lowest-achieving students. Placing struggling learners squarely in the academic mix with successful students is a sound practice for boosting achievement, self-esteem, and motivation.

Implementing Student Work Sessions

The student work session is the largest portion of each learning episode and provides time for students to work and practice. Student work sessions are structured strategically: before the session starts, the teacher delivers a compelling opener that piques interest and establishes purpose, and then leads a mini-lesson to model, explain, and deliver the information students need to engage in their assigned work during the rest of the period.

During the teacher-directed portion of a class period, it can be difficult to ascertain whether students are listening, daydreaming, understanding, or completely lost. When I am in classrooms, I typically calculate the percentage of students who are actively engaging during each component of the lesson. This is most difficult to do during the teacher-directed segment, because learners are often not doing anything except (we hope) listening. It's tough to observe evidence of student learning when teachers are doing the work.

One way to make this portion of the lesson more effective is to keep it to a manageable length. Direct instruction segments, Jensen (2005) asserts, should be brief because students are able to sit and listen effectively for only short periods. Figure 6.1 provides a guide for the appropriate duration of direct instruction at different grade bands, according to students' average attention spans. Even 12th grade teachers should not

FIGURE 6.1
Guidelines for Duration of Direct Instruction

Grade Level	Appropriate Duration of Direct Instruction
Grades K–2	5–8 minutes
Grades 3–5	8–12 minutes
Grades 6–8	12–15 minutes
Grades 9–12	12–15 minutes
Adult learners	15–18 minutes

Source: From *Teaching with the Brain in Mind* (p. 37), by E. Jensen, 2005, Alexandria, VA: ASCD. Copyright 2005 by ASCD.

talk for more than 15 minutes at a time, and they should break up that time by making notes and using strategies like graphic organizers and turn and tells.

In addition to keeping direct instruction times in line with attention spans, it is helpful to remember that introducing more than a few items during the lesson can be counterproductive. Sousa and Tomlinson (2011) remind us that the working memory hits its capacity at around four items. Information added past that point is largely rejected by the brain, and student frustration can set in.

After the direct instruction period, it's time for students to go to work. During this session, discussion and work shift onto students' shoulders. The teacher's role changes from front-of-the-room "deliverer" to middle-of-the-room "facilitator." As student academic talk increases and work progresses, it is paramount to monitor the quality of work and provide feedback that helps students advance toward the goal. This is the crucial time when students process and practice the standard.

Because student work sessions usually rely on cooperative learning, it is important to evaluate individual learning at the end of the period. Although cooperative learning enhances student achievement, teachers need to gauge not just how each group performed but also what each student knows. This assessment usually culminates the session quite smoothly, because the cooperative learning activities have built academic steam: students have processed and practiced new information with peers, engaged in vibrant conversations, and produced rigorous work. This work prepares them for both formative assessment and individual practice.

Strategies to Strengthen Reading Comprehension and Metacognition

We have established that effective student work sessions break down two key barriers to providing students with greater rigor and autonomy: behavior problems and lack of motivation. High-impact and engaging instruction, increased responsibility, and cooperative learning all improve students' behavior and motivation. The remaining barrier—low reading levels—is trickier to overcome. Fortunately, student work sessions present a perfect opportunity for students to strengthen their reading comprehension and practice metacognition, or thinking about thinking.

While students read, they need to become aware of their comprehension. Good readers connect to the words on a page, forming relationships with the text based on prior experiences. Perhaps these readers have done some reading on the topic already, heard about it on the news, or watched a movie with a similar theme. Harvey and Goudvis (2007) describe this process as "leaving tracks" (p. 28): making these connections enables readers to remember what they were thinking about while they read, which reinforces their comprehension and builds further connections to past and future learning.

One of the most counterproductive things we tell students is not to write in their books. We *want* them to write in their books—just not directly on the pages! Watch any proficient adult reader reading complex text, and you will see a pen or a highlighter moving across the page or notes being scribbled in the margin. To monitor and document their thinking, learners need to create notes of things that are important. If their task is to compare and contrast two ideas in a passage, for example, we cannot expect them to hang on to all those important points in their heads.

The following four strategies have clear benefits for cooperative as well as individual learning. They help students monitor their own comprehension, summarize key ideas, and stay engaged in and focused on their tasks. Rather than simply being assigned a passage, students know exactly why they are reading. Embedding these strategies also provides teachers with minute-by-minute access to students' thinking. In a cooperative learning setting, these techniques serve as visible evidence to team members that "I am doing my part." Taking these quick moments to document and organize their thoughts keeps students focused on the purpose of the task and prepares them to share with their peers. Eventually, students will be able to use these thinking tools to cite evidence and prepare their thoughts for writing.

VIP. This strategy, from Linda Hoyt (2009), works well as a way for students at all grade levels to document their thinking. I have experienced great success using this strategy in grades 3–12. When done well, VIP (which stands for "very important point") creates a bridge to complex tasks like writing and promotes robust conversations about student work.

Here's how it works. Students first create little sticky flags by cutting a sticky note into strips. As they come across an important point in their reading, they stick the flag right on the page and make a note on the flag. In a piece of fiction, for example, students may respond to a character's predicament. In social studies, students may jot down causes of a war. This structured approach to reading pays dividends when it comes time for students to share or write about their insights: they simply move the sticky flags to a sheet of paper or an anchor chart and arrange them depending on the task. If they are comparing and contrasting two concepts or people, for example, they can sort their notes into those two categories. After arranging the flags, students are an opening statement and a closing statement away from completing a compare and contrast piece of writing. Figure 6.2 (p. 102) shows what a "VIP'd" textbook page looks like, providing tangible evidence of students' reading and thinking.

Sticky notes. For tasks that require more note taking than sticky flags permit, using whole sticky notes works best. As students read, they take notes on the stickies. The small size of sticky notes, I have observed, makes the work seem more doable than taking notes on a large sheet of paper. In addition, students have only enough room to record the most important points, so they are compelled to keep focused on the task and make decisions about the purpose of the reading. For example, during a paired reading, each student can silently read a page or two and

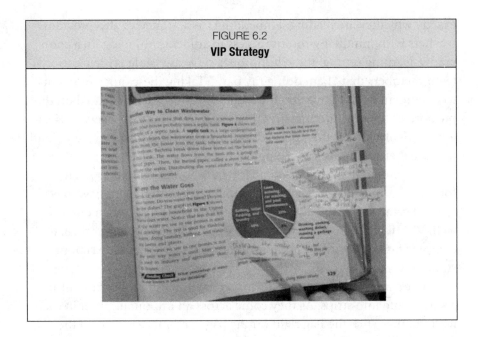

FIGURE 6.2
VIP Strategy

take notes on stickies. Next, the partners turn to each other and share their comments.

Highwriting. Another effective monitoring strategy is a combination of highlighting and note taking that I call *highwriting*. When a teacher simply provides students with highlighters, the result tends to be pages saturated with pink or yellow markings. The highwriting method encourages more judicious, thoughtful use of highlighting. When a reader decides that something is important enough to highlight, he or she makes a note in the margin summarizing the highlighted point. Every time students use the highlighter, they must make a corresponding note in the margin. In addition, only key phrases, not whole sentences, should be highlighted, and they must relate clearly to the purpose for reading. This practice works well with handouts, newspaper articles, and other similar texts, but obviously not textbooks.

Coding. Coding text is a monitoring strategy that works well for highly specific purposes. If, for example, two students are working together to explain the difference between kinetic and potential energy, the codes they use to mark the text might be *K* and *P*. A student searching for examples of figurative language in a text might use the codes *A, O,* and *S* to stand for *alliteration, onomatopoeia,* and *simile.* In deciphering fact from opinion, students might use *F* and *O.* Coding brings laser-like purpose to dense, often mundane reading and ensures that students remain aware of the task's purpose.

Strategies for Effective, Differentiated Student Work Sessions

Students come to school with a wide range of reading levels, but all are expected to demonstrate understanding of the same rigorous standards. Although this expectation poses challenges, it may be helpful to remember that lower-level readers go to the movies on the weekends and understand every nuance of complicated plots. They can understand complex concepts; they just need a little help on the reading. So teachers' goal is twofold: increasing students' reading proficiency while building their understanding of the standard.

With a little ingenuity and resourcefulness, adapting instruction for students at varying reading levels is quite doable. Cooperative learning lends itself well to differentiation, and having a partner or team for support can make all the difference to struggling students. To differentiate learning tasks for heterogeneous cooperative groups, teachers could

- Provide multiple sources of varying difficulty and interest.
- Provide short and longer passages on the same topic.
- Adjust the degree of text density (i.e., the frequency of unfamiliar words).
- Include supporting pictures and graphics with the text.
- Annotate the text with synonyms for unfamiliar words.
- Emphasize the purpose of the reading by marking certain parts of passages with "skip" or "important."
- Supplement the reading with short videos or audio recordings.
- Use literature circles that empower students to select their own readings.

Most of these suggestions can easily be incorporated into the following strategies, so keep them in mind as you read.

Paired Reading

Structured paired reading is a wonderful instructional tool that works for both fiction and nonfiction texts. "Paired reading" does not mean simply having students read or work with a partner. Rather, students make specific contributions to their pair (and sometimes to a larger group, such as a foursome).

Let's look at an example of an activity for paired reading of nonfiction, informational text. This earth science lesson's standard calls for students to compare and contrast the earth's core, mantle, and crust in terms of temperature, density, and composition. After sparking student curiosity and excitement with a compelling brainstorming opener (see Chapter 3 for more on success starters), the teacher posts anchor charts on the wall (see Figure 6.3)—one for each group of four. Each group then divides into two pairs.

FIGURE 6.3 Anchor Chart in Progress: Earth's Core, Mantle, and Crust			
	Temperature	**Density**	**Composition**
Core	6,000°C As hot as sun's surface	Twice as dense as mantle	Liquid outer core Solid inner core of iron and nickel
Mantle	Hotter than crust 500–4,000°C	2,900 km thick Denser than crust	More iron, magnesium, and calcium
Crust	Deeper gets hotter Up to 200°C	5 km–100 km deep Thinnest under oceans	Brittle and rigid Thin shell

Each pair decides which partner will initially take the role of reader and which will take the role of note taker. Sticky notes or "VIP" strips in hand, the note taker listens and follows along in the text as the reader reads. When a relevant detail, such as the temperature of the earth's core, comes up in the text, the note taker politely pauses the reader: "That's about the temperature of the core, so I need to jot down a note." (For younger students, the note taker can hold up a card showing a picture of a pause button.) The reader then continues. After a few paragraphs, the students reverse roles. Periodically, the partners lift their sticky notes from the pages of their text and relocate them to the appropriate spots on the anchor chart. Students literally stick their thinking right on their charts! It is helpful to distribute a different color of sticky note to each pair within a group of four, so that the thinking of each pair is discernible. By the time the pairs finish reading their passages, the anchor chart is covered with students' notes.

Next, each group of four assembles for a discussion of the reading. The cube strategy is great for facilitating this conversation. Students take turns rolling two cubes—one with *core, mantle,* and *crust* written on the sides, and the other with *temperature, density,* and *composition.* Each word should be doubled up so that all six sides of each cube are filled. Each student must explain to the group the combination that he or she rolled, referring to the group's anchor chart. For example, one student may explain everything about the density of the mantle. Another option is for group members to switch partners and solve a sort that contains the key elements of the reading, including pictures of the core, mantle, and crust. Each pair pieces together the sort using both the anchor chart and the classroom TIP chart.

This process makes learners' reading and thinking readily seen and heard. Students have read text, taken notes, drawn comparisons, and engaged in either discussion or classification of key elements of the topic. Students have now built up enough academic steam to be able to confidently undertake an individual task, such as completing a writing exercise about the concept. What would have happened if the assignment had simply been to "read pages 111–115 about the core, mantle, and crust"? For struggling or reluctant readers, simply assigning this passage would surely have produced weaker results.

Paired reading of fiction also offers many engaging opportunities. Students can act out characters' dialogue, read select portions chorally, or read sections silently and summarize them. They can predict what will happen next and visualize future scenes. In a lesson on the novel *Lord of the Flies*, for example, a pair may be tasked with comparing the characters of Piggy and Ralph. As they read, students may code relevant parts in the text *P* or *R* and record observations on a graphic organizer or anchor chart. Then, referring to the organizer or chart, partners can discuss how the characters are alike and different and how they change in response to plot developments. Another pair could analyze two other characters in the same way, and then both pairs could combine forces in a foursome.

The bow tie strategy is one that works especially well with both nonfiction and fiction paired readings, across all subject areas. For example, in a social studies paired reading, students could use the bow tie to compare two forms of government or two geographical regions; in math, to compare and contrast congruent and incongruent shapes; and in science, to compare and contrast two diseases or two parts of a cell.

If the learning goal of an English lesson on a fictional text is "How did these two characters respond to changes in circumstances?" each partner could take responsibility for one of the characters and record observations on his or her respective side of the bow tie, using sticky notes, a bulleted list, or a flowchart. The partners would then come together to discuss their findings and create a response for the center of the bow tie that demonstrates the pair's understanding of the learning goal. Students would pull information from both sides of the bow tie to cite as evidence for their combined answer.

An exercise in science class could ask pairs to come to a consensus on the question "Who is the most important scientist who has ever lived?" While one student reads about Albert Einstein, documenting her thinking along the way, her partner studies Sir Isaac Newton. After the partners finish their individual reading, they exchange evidence demonstrating the importance of their respective scientists. Students could also switch readings, so that they are experts on both scientists.

Walk the Line

For lessons that ask students to make a decision and cite evidence supporting their thinking, I encourage the use of a strategy I call *Walk the Line*. (And yes, in the classroom, I play a bit of the Johnny Cash song to cue the strategy.) First, the teacher runs masking tape across the floor in a line and then creates signs at either end of the line representing different choices. For the "most important scientist" question above, one end of the line would have a sign reading "Einstein" and the other end a sign reading "Newton," with a question mark in the middle of the line for students who are on the fence. Each pair would send a partner to the line with evidence to support the pair's argument. For other scenarios or topics of debate, the signs may read "Agree" and "Disagree" or "For" and "Against." As students argue their cases, other students on the line have the option to change their position.

In history, students can play the roles of historical figures they're reading about and present a topic from the figure's point of view. For example, in a class reading about the Trail of Tears, one student can come to the line as Andrew Jackson while another plays Sequoyah. What I appreciate about this strategy is that students have the opportunity to practice speaking, listening, critical thinking, and diplomacy skills.

Cooperative Learning Quadrants

Four is a logical number for cooperative groups. Placing students in groups of four enables pairs to convene with an adjacent pair to compare notes, discuss their work, and create a product. (Threes are workable but can be awkward because often two team members pair up and leave the third as, well, a third wheel.)

A highly effective strategy to use with groups of four is the cooperative learning quadrant. Each group owns a section of chart paper divided into quarters. This is the group's workstation, and all members write their names on it. Students use this area to make notes, attach sticky notes, illustrate concepts, create graphic organizers—whatever their task entails—but no matter which strategies they use, their thinking is evident throughout the process. Each member has a different role to play that is essential to the group task. These roles can be easily differentiated to tap into individual student talents and adjust for varying reading levels.

Figure 6.4 shows a cooperative learning quadrant for an 8th grade group tasked with creating a magazine cover that uses text and images to demonstrate the cotton gin's impact on slavery and the economy. The least proficient reader in the group takes on the role of the number cruncher, analyzing charts and graphs, while the most proficient reader assumes the role of biographer, which requires reading longer, dense text. The mid-level readers take on the roles of mechanical engineer and economist, which require them to engage with illustrated text that is roughly on grade level. The engineer examines drawings and explanations of how the cotton gin worked and shares his or her findings with the group, while the economist explains the phrase "King Cotton" and how the gin affected the economy of the United States and Great Britain. These group placements are strategic and planned in advance.

Learning quadrants place interesting, motivating work squarely on students' shoulders. The quadrants may include different characters from a story, causes of a war, types of energy, parts of cells, inventions, or animals. Students can read differently leveled works from the same author, take on the roles of four historical figures, or analyze different rocks. Although the individual tasks can be differentiated, the process is the same: each student has an important job to do that is essential to the group task. Thinking and evidence of learning are visible to both

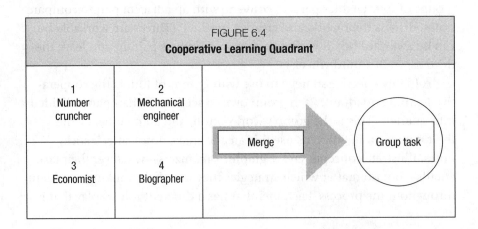

FIGURE 6.4
Cooperative Learning Quadrant

the group and the class, and students engage in robust conversations as they synthesize their research into one collaborative task or product. In addition to the group product, I typically conclude lessons with a short individual formative assessment to gather concrete evidence of student progress.

Jigsaws

One of the most common cooperative learning approaches is the jigsaw strategy, which breaks down a topic into pieces and then reconfigures it back into a whole. Each member of a cooperative group investigates a different category of a broader topic—for example, types of colonies, different food groups, different civilizations, various geographic regions, or even parts of fractions. The strength of the jigsaw is that students become "experts" in their designated fields and transmit their specialized knowledge to their teammates.

First, students convene in home groups and divide responsibilities. Teachers can assist in this process or let students choose their own topics. Next, each expert joins students from other groups who are investigating the same area. For example, in a jigsaw activity on the respiratory system, the four expert groups would include students learning about the nasal passage, the pharynx, the bronchi and lungs, and the larynx. The teacher assembles reading and other materials at four different expert areas around the room, clearly marked with signs. Each expert area should include a variety of materials to allow for differentiation. It may also be beneficial to cue up a short informational video for each expert group. Within their expert groups, students share materials, take notes on key points, and discuss their findings.

Next, armed with knowledge, the experts return to their home groups to teach their portion of the lesson to the group. Students should use a graphic organizer for note taking, such as a flip chart. After each expert has taught his or her topic, the group collaborates on a task that encompasses each component of the jigsaw. For the respiratory system jigsaw, for example, students might create a flowchart using text and pictures to explain how the respiratory system works. Groups who wrap up early might get an additional task, such as coming up with a metaphor for the respiratory system.

Learning Stations

Learning stations are another effective strategy to use during student work sessions. The benefits of learning stations are significant. For one, they incorporate movement into the lesson, which, as Jensen (2005) notes, gives students more energy and brainpower to perform well academically. In addition, students are more likely to exhibit on-task behavior while working at learning stations than they are during traditional seatwork (Day & Drake, 1986). Novelty is another factor that makes stations successful: the brain increases its focus when it engages in novel activities (Sousa & Tomlinson, 2011). Even when a student doesn't find a station engaging, something new is right around the bend.

Teachers can easily customize learning stations for a variety of learning styles. A kinesthetic word sort, a short video, a technology component—when constructed appropriately, stations can truly offer something for every learner. Before getting carried away with creative ideas, however, teachers should keep in mind that their purpose is to move students toward mastery of the learning objective. Novelty alone isn't enough; the tasks must have purpose and meaning, too. Fun should never supplant rigor. Some ideas for effective learning station activities that suit a variety of learning styles include vocabulary games, labs and demonstrations, error analysis, and map skills exercises (e.g., having students locate specific longitudes and latitudes on a map). Activities can incorporate a diverse array of materials that also work for various learning styles, such as concrete representations; leveled reading passages; videos (cued up so students just push "play"); primary sources, such as letters, budgets, or ship's logs; pictures (either digital or hard-copy); picture books (even for secondary students!); and editorials.

Learning stations are often defined as a co-teaching structure, for good reason: they offer a great opportunity for co-teachers to distribute their talents. Students can receive feedback from both teachers, and both teachers can participate in the hands-on, differentiated activities with students. Learning stations are quite doable with one teacher in the room, however, and they are versatile in other ways, too. They can be used both for cooperative learning experiences and for independent work. In addition, although they have long been the domain of elementary classrooms and physical education departments, they are perfect for secondary-level content-area classrooms. For example, learning stations for a health unit on nutrition may ask students to

- Examine fast-food advertisements and produce a written response to the ads' approaches.
- Examine food product labels and calculate percentages of fat, vitamins, and so on.
- Watch a short video on nutrition and create a PowerPoint slide including key points.
- Complete a sort of vocabulary words for the unit.
- Choose a short passage from a selection of texts on the topic to read, and take notes on sticky notes.
- As a culminating task, create a nutritious menu for their family for the week.

Before students begin rotating through the stations, the teacher should briefly model expectations for each station and make sure to leave written instructions (or have a student who has completed the station help get the next group started). I find that it's helpful for students to carry an organizer with them to document their journey.

Learning stations are a mainstay of 8th grade math teacher Ms. Ruis's instruction. Her students have significant academic challenges, but you'd never know it from the type of work they get to do. Ms. Ruis notes that "whole-group instruction is not impactful for my kids, and they hate worksheets." Instead, her students engage in highly focused stations three to four days of the week. "When I start talking too much is when I lose them, so I let them do a lot of the talking."

When the bell rings, Ms. Ruis explains to students the big picture of the day's concept and models what to do at each station. Each station is also equipped with clear instructions for the task. One station is teacher-assisted so that Ms. Ruis can help each student individually, but the rest are self-regulatory. At one station, students used a catapult to learn about scatter plots, while another station had students complete a vocabulary sort. The technology station typically reviews prerequisite skills students need to grasp the current concept. The stations vary and typically last for two days. A few minutes before class ends, students gather again for a formative assessment and clarification of misconceptions.

Menus

A menu is a tool that lets students decide how they want to demonstrate their learning. According to research (Bomia et al., 1997), giving students some control over their learning is an essential component in enhancing student motivation. For students, being in an academic downward spiral can bring a sense of futility and lack of control. Increasing students' sense of control by giving them choices can rebuild their belief that they can be successful. The first time I ever implemented a menu, an astonished student asked, "Do you mean I can pick which ones I want to do?"

Carefully constructed menus can be strikingly effective. First, they are by their nature crafted for differentiation. In addition to the choices they provide, they enable students to complete tasks at varying times, since they won't all be working on the same tasks in the same order. This allows teachers to give students timely, private feedback that gives learners the opportunity to improve their work and earn a higher grade.

Using menus may necessitate an adjustment in both teacher and student thinking. Students who are accustomed to more teacher-directed classrooms might show some initial uncertainty at having this level of academic freedom, whereas teachers may be unclear on what their part is. A talented language arts teacher recently asked me for some ideas for his last period of the day. Teaching 7th graders at 3:30 p.m. poses special challenges for even the best-equipped educator. The class was reading *The Outsiders* by S. E. Hinton, and lessons that had been effective earlier in the day were failing to hold students' attention as afternoon buses rolled by the windows. Together, we created a menu for the assigned chapter that gave students a choice of several tasks incorporating a variety of learning styles and interests. We even let students decide how they wanted to read—alone, with a partner, or with the teacher. As we looked out over the classroom, we saw one student on the computer researching cars from the 1960s, one girl tucked in the corner reading quietly, and still others working together drawing a plot line on chart paper.

The teacher leaned over and asked me, "So what am *I* supposed to do?"

Sometimes, the mark of a brilliant lesson is how little students need us.

Menus can be elaborately designed with appetizers, entrees, and desserts, or very simply structured in a list or chart format. A block menu is a straightforward approach: learners simply circle their choice for each task and can typically begin anywhere. Figure 6.5 shows a block menu that includes visual, auditory, and kinesthetic tasks for a lesson on juvenile justice.

A couple of caveats: as teachers design their menus, they must ensure that any combination of tasks chosen will enable students to meet the learning objective. Although the creative aspect can be captivating for students, it is equally important to establish that students are mastering the standard. In my experience, I have found that menu use should not extend more than a couple of days at a time: in addition to maintaining the novelty of the strategy, using the menu on a short-term basis allows for timely goal completion and feedback.

FIGURE 6.5
Block Menu: Juvenile Justice

Learning Task	Option 1	Option 2	Option 3	Feedback
Compare and contrast *delinquent* and *unruly* behavior.	Create your own organizer that demonstrates the similarities and differences, and the consequences of each.	Create a Venn diagram that illustrates the similarities and differences, and the consequences of each.	Create a matrix that demonstrates the similarities and differences, and the consequences of each.	__/40 points
Describe the rights of juveniles in custody.	Create a chart that describes these rights.	Create a short PSA that describes these rights.	Create a sort that categorizes these rights.	__/40 points
Demonstrate knowledge of vocabulary: *intake, detention, juvenile,* and *delinquent.*	Create word art for each word.	Write a definition for and draw a picture of each word.	Create a flip chart for the words that includes each word, its definition, and a picture.	__/20 points

2-5-8 Menu

I first saw this jewel of a menu in a math menu book by Laurie West-phal (2009) and have since adapted it for every subject area. Students can choose various combinations of tasks that are worth 2, 5, or 8 points (depending on difficulty level) to reach 10 points. The wonderfully motivational element is that it feels so *doable*. One student can select one 8 and one 2, while another can choose two 5s, and a struggling student can choose five 2s. A 2-point math question may require fewer steps than a 5-pointer, which may involve fractions or messier numbers. In language arts, a 2-pointer may ask students to identify parts of speech, while a 5-point question requires them to come up with examples of different parts of speech or to compare and contrast two parts of speech. Eight-point questions in all subjects involve higher-level, abstract, or out-of-the-box thinking.

One caveat with 2-5-8 menus: students who accept the 8-point challenge risk scoring just a 2 if they miss it. One solution is to craft a question that has multiple answers; another is to offer a "lifeline" that gives students a second chance, such as a similar sample problem to complete. At his or her discretion, the teacher can offer bonus questions that enable students to make up for questions they answered incorrectly.

Four Practices to Consider Dropping

We have looked at numerous strategies for creating effective, engaging, collaborative student work sessions. To make room for these powerful practices, we may want to reassess the effectiveness of some current strategies we use. In particular, the following practices, although widely used, warrant scrutiny.

Assign and Tell

This practice, referred to by Vacca and Vacca (2002) as "assign and tell" (p. 6), increases in frequency from elementary to secondary grades. Essentially, the teacher tells students to read a textbook passage and complete the questions at the end. Students copy a few lines from the textbook to answer each question. Teachers often wind up giving students a summary of what they read and calling on students for the predictable answers to the questions. The most engaged person in this scenario is quite possibly the teacher, who is in the unenviable role of "giver of all information." Assign and tell omits one of the most important motivational aspects of reading: purpose. In addition, beyond the few lines transcribed from the textbook, where is the actual evidence that students even read the passage?

Round Robin Reading

Round robin reading is a common practice in which students read aloud in turn, often from textbooks. For such a frequently used strategy, it gets scant support from research. One study (Eldredge, Reutzel, & Hollingsworth, 1996) found that students in a round robin group performed more poorly in vocabulary acquisition, word recognition, reading fluency, reading comprehension, and word analysis than students using a shared reading approach.

In addition, students don't even end up reading much in a round robin setting. Pearson and Gallagher (1983) found that in most upper-elementary classrooms using round robin, students read only about a page apiece, while the teacher interspersed the reading with low-level questions. And Armbruster and colleagues (1991) found that each student typically read no more than a paragraph during round robin practice.

For low-achieving students in particular, round robin reading is problematic. While one student reads, what are the rest doing? There is often no observable evidence of thinking, comprehension, or engagement during this process. And because students read at different paces, while one student reads aloud, the more proficient readers are forced to slow down while weaker ones have difficulty staying on track.

Finally, there is the issue of the sheer inhumanity of putting weaker readers on display in front of their peers, with every miscue often being publicly corrected. The process may be equally torturous for higher-achieving readers, who must wait, wait, wait for their one turn to read a short passage.

Popcorn Reading

A particularly brutal cousin of round robin reading is popcorn reading. The goal of popcorn reading is primarily to embarrass your friends.

One student reads for a while and then at a sneaky moment—perhaps in the middle of a hyphenated word at the end of a line—says "Popcorn!" and calls on an unsuspecting classmate who is probably experiencing a momentary lapse of attention. That red-faced student has obviously lost his place in the text, so the first reader calls on another victim, perhaps the student who just returned from the nurse with a blazing fever.

Popcorn reading fails to realize any purpose in reading; the strategy's goal is simply to get a text read. Deep comprehension is difficult in this setting, with students reading small snippets and breaking at the most illogical spots. I am in total agreement with Donalyn Miller, author of *The Book Whisperer* (2009), who describes the process thusly: "The popcorn popper continues, readers burn out one by one, and comprehension breaks down for everyone in the room" (p. 147).

Never-Ending Tasks

In an attempt to instill rigor, teachers sometimes simply make assignments longer or have students do "more." In fact, less is usually more. Students' brains have limited capacities for storage. Sousa (2008) recommends thinking in terms of segments, or chunks: 12- to 15-minute segments for elementary classrooms and 15- to 20-minute segments for secondary classrooms. Although the class period may be 60 or 90 minutes long, 20-minute segments allow for more learning because the brain does not get overloaded. This is partly why learning stations, paired readings, carousels, bow ties, and other strategies in this book work so well.

"Less is more" applies to assignment length, too. Long worksheets actually provide an opportunity for students to disappear in class. In contrast, making notes on chart paper taped to the wall, rotating through timed stations, and working in cooperative groups increase student visibility and provide immediate opportunities for feedback.

Reflections on Student Work Sessions

Getting low-achieving students to consistently work toward their own academic improvement is a challenge, to be sure. But the path often taken—giving them more seatwork, less rigor, and less interaction—is the opposite of what will move students academically.

In his bestselling book *Flow*, Mihaly Csikszentmihalyi (1990) analyzes the conditions that lead to the mental "flow" state, where we are completely and single-mindedly absorbed in the task at hand. In the classroom, students who are in the flow state are so immersed in a lesson or activity that they can't believe the bell just rang. These students are not asking, "Is this for a grade?" They're asking, "Can we stay longer?"

Two conditions of the flow experience are stretching to accomplish something worthwhile and pursuing realistic goals. Students' skills must be adequate for the instructional challenge in front of them. Another factor that contributes to this intense level of concentration is access to immediate, clear feedback. With achievable, worthwhile tasks and immediate feedback, the student work session is ripe with opportunities for flow.

Student work sessions look different from traditional classes. Students work together and monitor their progress. Their textbooks are covered in sticky notes. They move; they discuss; they create. At every turn, we see their thinking and respond to it. So do their classmates. The strategies in this chapter pull students into the academic fold rather than quarantining them in remediation. And while they may not make it to *Jeopardy* . . . you never know.

Checklist for student work sessions:

❏   Students demonstrate their thinking.

❏   Instruction and texts are differentiated for varying reading levels.

❏   Students play active roles in the learning process.

❏   Conversations about the standard are robust.

❏   Learning integrates new vocabulary.

❏   Cooperative learning is structured.

❏   Tasks provide choice for students.

❏   Work and conversations are supported by evidence of learning.

❏   Grouping is strategic and effective.

❏   Feedback is immediate and moves work upward.

❏   Work strictly adheres to the standard or learning goal.

7

Student Motivation: Creating Engaging Tasks and a Positive Learning Environment

"I can't get Sonia to do *anything* in my class," one teacher confides to another during lunch. "She is barely passing, and today I caught her reading a library book instead of doing her work."

"Really? I find that hard to believe. Sonia is one of my hardest-working students! I even count on her to help the other students."

"Well, that's weird. Hmm."

This conversation, which has probably taken place in every school in the country, speaks to the heart of student motivation. The same student can thrive in one subject and barely cling to life in another. Even within the confines of a single lesson, students' motivation ebbs and flows. On-task behavior can quickly disintegrate into disinterest. A student who is genuinely engaged in adding a series of fractions may shut down when the work switches to word problems. Another student may be completely enthralled in a lab activity but take a nap during silent reading.

What causes one student to jump in with gusto and another not to bother bringing a pencil? Motivation or its lack stems from complex messages and questions that students' brains are sending them: "Does the assignment have enough value to make it worth my effort? If I do try, will I be successful? How will I save face if I fail? Is the task too easy or out of reach?"

Motivation = Value + Confidence

Student motivation is somewhat situational, depending largely on the value students assign to a task and their perceptions of their own capability to successfully complete the task. According to Hansen (1989), when value and confidence are both high, learners are likely to be engaged and motivated. Conversely, when value and confidence are both low, students may completely reject a task. Schunk and Meece (2006) found that students are likely to engage in activities that they believe will have positive outcomes and avoid activities they believe will have negative outcomes.

To begin the process of understanding what moves students to become genuinely engaged and what may trigger less desirable behaviors, evaluate your own level of motivation for the following tasks by indicating the level of value or relevance each task holds for you and the level of confidence you have in your ability to successfully complete the task.

Task One: Working in teams, determine your school's environmental footprint this year. Evaluate the school's water, gas, and electricity usage and cafeteria waste. Interview operational employees of the district to ascertain the district's environmental goals, and compare your school with others in the area. Make recommendations to the superintendent based on your discoveries.

Value: high, medium, low   *Confidence*: high, medium, low

Task Two: You and your friend are visiting the Empire State Building. You think it would be comical to drop pennies on strangers' heads as they walk down the street. You both drop a handful of pennies from the top (443 meters). With a partner, calculate the time it will take the pennies to land.

Value: high, medium, low   *Confidence*: high, medium, low

Task Three: On your own, copy the dictionary definitions of 25 vocabulary words from the unit. Create a sentence for each word.

Value: high, medium, low   *Confidence*: high, medium, low

The first task, which is a lesson I have implemented, holds a high degree of value for most learners. In addition, the description does not indicate that there will be any skill or knowledge barriers, so confidence is also usually high. Students' brains are signaling to them, "This is interesting and relevant, and I can do it. I'm going to jump right in!"

The second task may have value or interest for students, but some students may not feel confident enough in their math skills to complete it. Students may genuinely want to participate in the lesson but feel uncertain about how to be successful. However, the social element—in this case, working with a partner—can enhance self-confidence and, as a result, motivation.

The third task is tedious and holds little personal value. Although most students would feel confident in their ability to successfully complete this assignment, few will feel genuinely motivated to do so. Students may go through the motions for a while, or daydream or doodle a bit. Some will choose to complete it. Others may simply copy a friend's work on the bus ride home. Who cares? Their perception of the assignment's value is so low that it just doesn't seem to matter.

Hansen's (1989) three-year study of almost 200 elementary school students in bilingual classes identified four behavioral tactics that students employ as they weigh the value of a task against their perceived ability to be successful: *engaging, dissembling, evading,* and *rejecting.* Each of these tactics acts as a means of self-protection from failure, and all of the students observed in the study engaged in each of the four tactics at some point. Figure 7.1 provides a rundown of what each of these tactics looks like.

Thus, as teachers are explaining today's task, students are making important decisions about their course of action. Does the task hold enough value to warrant a sustained commitment? Do students feel confident enough about their potential for success to embark on the task? In other words, are the benefits worth the risk of failure?

Students' answers to these questions are not made in a vacuum. If we want students to find *value* in a task, we must thoughtfully construct that task to provide the right level of challenge and interest. If we want students to feel *confident,* we must create a learning environment that fosters their self-efficacy and makes them feel safe enough to take academic risks. Let's look at why self-efficacy is so important.

FIGURE 7.1
Behavioral Tactics Students Use

Likely Conditions	Lesson Tactic	Student Behaviors Observed
• Value high • Self-confidence high	Lesson engaging	• Attempts to resolve unfamiliar aspects • Searches for accuracy • Feels confident in meeting demands
• Value high • Self-confidence low	Lesson dissembling	• Pretends to understand or be busy • Makes excuses
• Value low • Self-confidence high	Lesson evading	• Sees little reason to engage in task • Exhibits off-task behaviors such as talking or going through motions
• Value low • Self-confidence low	Lesson rejecting	• Withdraws from lesson or is passive • Exhibits anger

Source: From "Lesson Evading and Lesson Dissembling: Ego Strategies in the Classroom," by D. Hansen, 1989, *American Journal of Education,* *97*(2), pp. 184–208. Copyright 1989 by the University of Chicago.

Why Self-Efficacy Matters

Self-efficacy refers to individuals' judgments about their capabilities to perform at a certain level (Bandura, 1984). Because students' own negative beliefs about themselves stand in the way of their motivation and success, it's important to find ways to support their self-efficacy.

Self-efficacy has implications that go beyond a student's decision whether or not to engage in a task. Self-efficacious individuals tend to persist longer, participate more readily, and work harder (Schunk & Meece, 2006). In addition, self-efficacious students show greater perseverance during adversity, are more optimistic, have less anxiety, and achieve more than do students who lack self-efficacy. It makes sense, then, that self-efficacy is a significant predictor of academic achievement in students across all content areas and grade levels (Usher & Pajares, 2008). In fact, 25 percent of the variance in the prediction of academic performance relates to self-efficacy (Pajares, 2006).

Unfortunately, students who have inadequate levels of self-efficacy often exhibit less-healthy behaviors than their more confident peers do. As Figure 7.1 demonstrated, low confidence can thwart success and promote off-task behaviors. According to Brophy (2010), students who perceive themselves as incapable tend to avoid academic situations in which they may fail, or give up easily at the first sign of frustration. They withdraw from participation and instead focus on masking their confusion to save face. They even have an increased propensity toward pessimism, stress, and depression (Pajares, 2006). In addition, self-efficacy tends to decrease as students get older. Declines are especially evident around 7th grade, when students are making the difficult transition from elementary school to secondary school and facing significant changes in grading, peers, and classes (Schunk & Meece, 2006).

Sadly, the very students who need to dig deep, persevere, and overcome obstacles to mount an academic comeback tend to do the opposite. This downward trend is exacerbated by the stress often experienced by struggling students.

The Trouble with Stress

Small amounts of stress are inevitable and can even enhance performance, but high levels of stress and anxiety are toxic to learning. Imagine being pulled over by the police on a dark road late at night. Passing motorists glare at you through the blinding blue lights, certain that you have been up to no good. The officer runs your tag. Panic sweeps through your veins as you try to recall whether you paid the car insurance this month. As the officer returns to your window, he props his hand on his gun holster. Now imagine trying to solve some calculus problems or interpret an abstruse passage from Shakespeare in your current state of mind.

Stress and anxiety are enemies of self-efficacy and learning. In fact, students can even mistake their own apprehension in class for a lack of competence in the content (Usher & Pajares, 2008). When a student experiences negative stress, his or her brain releases increased cortisol, known as the stress hormone, and focuses on helping the student survive the situation. The learning objective quickly becomes secondary. This reaction is fundamental to human survival, but it is not conducive to learning. When a student is experiencing anxiety, the information being taught does not make it to the higher thinking centers of the brain, and if this period of high stress is prolonged, new information is unlikely to be processed or stored (Willis, 2006).

Students with high levels of anxiety in math, Ashcraft and Kirk (2001) found, made more errors in mental addition, demonstrated increased reaction time, and had lower levels of available working memory than did students with lower levels of stress. Even when their answers were correct, it took longer for students to get there. The authors suggest that anxiety triggers an instinctive response to the student's worries that overrides thinking about the math at hand. In other words, the brain is redirected to solve the anxiety problem rather than the math problem. The result is a slowdown of math processing and diminished accuracy.

On the other hand, when students are in a low-stress learning environment, their brains release feel-good endorphins that have the opposite effect of cortisol. Sousa and Tomlinson (2011) explain that this favorable response to the situation makes learning and remembering information easier. Students who are feeling positive about learning enjoy more focus and read and write more effectively. Creativity, problem solving, patience, and social behaviors improve as well (Willis, 2006). In a sense, the body encourages success by releasing a feel-good chemical that becomes associated with it: students want to get more of that feeling!

Building Student Motivation

Motivation is the key factor to turning around struggling students' performance. However, building students' motivation is not a separate program or system. It hinges on giving relevant, engaging tasks and providing a safe learning environment. Putting these factors in place signals to students that if they put in a sustained effort, they have a high probability of reaching a positive outcome. The following sections provide strategies that will help you create the conditions for student motivation to flourish in your own classroom.

Creating Tasks That Genuinely Engage Students

There is a direct correlation between the nature of the tasks teachers give students and students' self-efficacy and potential academic success.

The way we design our tasks can motivate students or derail them. It's up to us. Interesting, relevant tasks that hold an appropriate level of challenge bring opportunities for success, whereas meaningless or unchallenging assignments lead only to demotivation and even failure. The following guidelines will help you ensure that the tasks you give build students' motivation and confidence.

Make it relevant and interesting. In an attempt to give lower-achieving students something they can do, teachers may assign tedious seatwork that lacks creativity or purpose, such as worksheets. However, little satisfaction results from accomplishing something of little worth, and such tasks set students up for demotivation and off-task behavior. It's not just struggling learners who find irrelevant, unchallenging lessons demotivating; stronger students will also turn to more interesting things—looking at their cell phones, writing notes, or doodling—during boring lessons. The difference is that higher-performing students can generally evade for a large chunk of class time, scramble at the end of class, and still manage to pull something together to turn in (Hansen, 1989). Weaker students who evade are more likely to leave without putting their assignment in the box.

Because the brain is always scanning for what is meaningful, students' attention will naturally be diverted to what is personally relevant, which may not be the lesson. Therefore, truly effective, engaging tasks must be interesting and relevant to students' lives. Bomia and colleagues (1997) found that assigning projects that personally benefit students and have practical applications increases student effort. If the standard is about banking, for example, the teacher can design a task that has students select a local bank to open an account with based on information they collect from banks' websites. Students can cite arguments for why they chose this particular bank. If a health standard relates to managing stress, the teacher could have students chart their stress levels for a day. If a class is learning about the Bill of Rights, students could take on the roles of our nation's founders and create their own bill of rights, then compare and contrast it with the actual document.

Provide an appropriate level of difficulty. In addition to building interest and relevance into tasks, teachers should put thought into tasks' level of difficulty. A task offering the right degree of challenge inspires students, while tasks that are either too easy or too difficult tend to disengage students. A task that is too easy can bring tedium and boredom, whereas a task that is too difficult or unreachable for many students can increase stress, lower self-efficacy, and result in embarrassment. It is more effective to scaffold a stimulating, challenging task that requires students to stretch their skills than to provide overly simple assignments that lack value.

Incorporate choice and social interaction. Students gauge their potential involvement in activities according to their likelihood of succeeding or failing, which is one reason why menus and cooperative learning are so effective: tasks that provide students with choices and allow them to interact increase students' chances of success and foster engagement.

When students slip into a failure cycle and display unproductive behaviors, teachers sometimes respond by shifting their focus from student-centered to teacher-directed instruction in an attempt to manage classroom behaviors. Placing greater restrictions on students' intellectual freedom, however, may inadvertently contribute to students' sense that they have little control over their academic futures. According to Ames (1992), offering small choices throughout lessons increases students' motivation and perceptions of autonomy. Choices also encourage students to take greater responsibility for their own learning (Stipek & Weisz, 1981). Menus, for example, enable students to select the task that they believe will result in a positive outcome. Every student's product may be different, but the teacher will know that each student has genuinely engaged in the standard. Teachers can let students make all kinds of choices: which writing prompt they would like to respond to, the order in which they complete tasks, which practice problems or homework questions to work on, and so on.

Students are social creatures, so tasks that incorporate social interactions make learning more meaningful. Research (Johnson et al., 1981) has established that structured, thoughtfully designed cooperative learning promotes academic achievement and productivity. When a student has an important job to do within an interdependent group, he or she feels an increased responsibility and motivation to perform to a higher level (Johnson & Johnson, 2009).

Don't forget openers. Small, frequent successes increase students' self-efficacy (Bomia et al., 1997). It bears repeating that well-crafted success starters that ignite intellectual curiosity and get all students actively engaged can pay dividends throughout class. For struggling learners in particular, this spark of immediate success can boost self-efficacy right from the get-go and set the tone for engagement. Beginning class with a passive, review-oriented warm-up may serve as a predictable classroom ritual but does little for student engagement. The opening minutes are crucial in addressing the age-old question "What's this got to do with me?"

Creating an Inspired, Safe Learning Environment

We can easily make the case that students who are struggling academically are suffering from high levels of stress. It's like a bad version of the movie *Groundhog Day*: every day, the bus arrives to take students to the place where they are unsuccessful. There is no way out. As adults, we have options when we're not doing well: we can change jobs, move, possibly start over. Although from our perspective, students have some control over their achievement—they can try harder and get to school on time, for example—low-achieving students' perception is often one of futility. Caught in a world of anxiety and failure, their brains stay focused on coping and survival rather than critical thinking and academic success.

To counteract students' negative thinking about school, it is vital that schools provide a learning space that is nurturing and safe. Students who are concerned about self-protection and hiding their academic shortfalls need to feel safe enough to ask questions and share their work. A positive, inspired learning environment that enhances thinking, memory, participation, and self-efficacy can only help students understand concepts and succeed the first time.

The safe classroom is a welcoming place in which mistakes are part of learning, feedback is ongoing and productive, classroom management is predictable, and students have some autonomy over their learning. Students are willing to take the risk of going out on a learning limb in such an environment. The following strategies will encourage academic achievement and self-confidence and build intrinsic motivation in students.

Make a positive connection with students right away. The opening minutes of class should set a welcoming mood. Teachers' words and demeanor should communicate, "I'm so glad you're here!" rather than "Why are you late again?" It's important to plant positive seeds right from the start by smiling, greeting each student by name, and starting instruction on a personal note ("I thought of you when I was developing this lesson. . . ."). In addition, consider making a retreat from the "Pencil Wars"—that is, penalizing students for coming unprepared. Instead, establish a system that enables students to discreetly check out a pencil for the day. Avoid the temptation to charge collateral for a 10-cent pencil by holding students' phones, keys, or the promise of a kidney if you ever need one. The opening minutes of class need to be positive, particularly for students who dread coming to school.

Model mistakes as a positive step toward learning. Whether we're rewriting papers, fixing errors, or adjusting a layup shot, we know that making and correcting mistakes make us better. But for the struggling learner, mistakes can be humiliating. To avoid embarrassment or loss of face, students may prefer to skip a challenging learning task (Sousa & Tomlinson, 2011). It's up to teachers to model to students that mistakes are a natural and helpful part of the learning process. When we make an error, rather than quipping, "Just seeing if you were paying attention!" we should own up to it: "My subject and verb don't agree in that sentence; help me think that through," or "I am not sure I'm pronouncing that river's name correctly, so let me check on that." Modeling the process of collaboratively investigating the source of the error and thinking about the problem in a different way teaches students how to overcome mistakes. Modeling mistakes in other areas helps students as well. Having a rough day in the classroom? Model gracious civility and apologize privately when you handle a classroom situation in a regrettable manner. Students can learn from watching how teachers handle awkward situations.

Group students thoughtfully. Purposeful grouping of students has numerous benefits. For one, although too much teacher assistance may signal a lack of confidence in the learner's ability (Schunk & Meece, 2006), there is no such negative effect associated with peer assistance. On the contrary, strategic grouping can promote struggling students' self-efficacy by giving them a vicarious sense of success. Students gain confidence by observing other students being successful at a task (Usher & Pajares, 2008). This experience can prompt students to think, "Hey, I may be able to do this as well!" On the other hand, grouping two struggling students together in a task may have the reverse effect ("No one can do this!") and reduce self-efficacy.

It works best to pair a student whose skill in a given concept is still emerging with a more proficient student who also enjoys working with others. As a rule, I do not group students at the highest level of mastery with those who are struggling the most; that gap is just too wide.

Strategic grouping can also be based on factors other than academic progress. For example, a student who exhibits a high degree of tenacity could be grouped with a student who tends to shut down at the first sign of trouble. Struggling students benefit from working with peers who model good coping skills (Brophy, 2010) because they can see the thought processes and strategies that successful students use to overcome difficulties.

Communicate that students control their own academic destinies. Stipek and Weisz (1981) contend that students' perceptions of the *causes* of success or failure are potentially as important as their *actual* success or failure. Thus, having a sense of control over events can spur students' academic achievement. Teachers should cultivate students' awareness that perseverance and effort correlate directly with success. Praising students for simply being "smart" can signal that intelligence is innate and unchangeable (Pajares, 2006) and success is out of students' control. It's better to meet with students privately to go over specific areas in which they were missing a few key points or could have used a certain strategy and to show them what success looks like: "See how you cited evidence in that portion? It's left out in this part. More support in this area will strengthen your argument." Construct a success scenario for students, showing them how they can fix problem areas with a little more work or by taking a different direction, and letting them know that you have confidence in their abilities (Brophy, 2010).

Establish short-term goals. In addition to working toward the overarching learning goals on the standards wall, students benefit from having short-term goals, which build self-efficacy (Pajares, 2006). It always feels good to complete something successfully, however small. Check-off sheets, to-do lists, and agendas show students evidence of their progress. It is helpful to keep in mind that students' sense of time is different from ours. Planning for the future for elementary school students extends about three days, middle school students roughly two weeks, and high school students about a month (Mendler, 2000). While we are planning for retirement, they are wondering if it's tater-tot day in the cafeteria. And although it's natural to want to help students develop long-term goals, accomplishing short-term goals fosters student motivation.

Provide positive feedback. We already know that providing frequent, timely, specific feedback contributes to student success. It is also important to praise what is praiseworthy and recognize and post successful work. Write students personal notes when you are impressed with their work, their contributions to class discussions, or their ideas for a paper. Encouragement can raise self-efficacy, particularly when it comes from a trusted source. On that note, one caveat: disingenuous praise can lessen our credibility, so avoid giving false accolades or promises. What happens if we tell a student we're certain she will ace a test, and she fails it?

Elicit feedback from students. It may seem scary, but when I am in schools, I frequently solicit student feedback about lessons. This gives students a sense of agency over their learning and shows them that their thoughts are heard and valued. Getting feedback can be as simple as having students anonymously submit sticky notes describing one thing they especially liked about the lesson and one thing they think should change for the next class. Here is an example of a quick open-response survey I have used: (a) This part of the lesson worked well for me: _____. (b) This would help me learn better: _____. One student recently wrote, "I liked getting to put the sticky flags on the map to show the east. Sometimes, I would like to get out of my desk for a minute." I am always taken aback by how thoughtful and specific students are, and, typically, by the kindness they show.

Provide evenhanded responses to classroom situations. Although students benefit from lessons that incorporate excitement and novelty, when it comes to classroom management, they need dependability. Overreacting to infractions, trying to catch students off guard to publicly display their lapses in attention, or having obvious class favorites diminishes student motivation and can add undue stress to the class-room (Brophy, 2010). Teacher practices like these can prompt students to engage in protecting their self-worth at the expense of learning. In contrast, establishing reliable routines and responding to problems in a fair-minded way foster students' trust and prime them for learning.

Nurture your own self-efficacy. There is a correlation between teach-ers' level of self-efficacy and their students' motivation. Teachers with high self-confidence work with students, particularly lower achievers, more effectively than do teachers who have lower levels of self-efficacy. Hoy and Davis (2006) indicate that teachers who have a high degree of self-efficacy are more persistent and work harder than their colleagues do. They are also more likely to give students adequate response times, set challenging and proximal goals for students, and confidently teach students with academic difficulties. In addition, self-efficacious teachers tend to have a greater belief in their students' academic capabilities, and they tend not to see students' potential as fixed. Their confidence in their teaching abilities enables them to give students more academic control, and they even exude more warmth to frustrated students than their less efficacious colleagues do.

"What Are You Going to Give Me?"
The Problem with Extrinsic Motivation

An obvious omission from the list of strategies that enhance student motivation is the use of extrinsic or tangible rewards. Incentives such as pizza parties, candy, and gold stars subtly communicate that students would never dream of doing these awful school tasks on their own, so they need to be bribed. Unfortunately, extrinsic rewards may actually prove detrimental to students' learning.

According to Deci, Koestner, and Ryan (2001), tangible rewards usually have the opposite of their intended effect. Although they may control students' immediate behaviors, they can negatively influence student performance on subsequent tasks. Learners are likely to show less persistence and interest in tackling challenging tasks. The researchers found that when students received rewards for simply engaging in a task or for completing a task, their intrinsic motivation declined. Rewards tied to performance also resulted in a decline in intrinsic motivation. The one area in which tangible rewards did *not* inhibit motivation was when the tasks were dull. The researchers theorized that in these cases, students had no intrinsic motivation to begin with.

Providing tangible rewards may actually have a negative impact on long-term student motivation (except, possibly, when it comes to skills that require a significant amount of drill and practice). Best-selling business author Daniel Pink (2009) compares extrinsic rewards with a jolt of caffeine: in the short term, it will probably get you going, but after the caffeine buzz wears off, you may feel less motivated than before. The one reward that has been proven to work is verbal praise, which increases intrinsic motivation in students (Deci et al., 2001) much more than tangible rewards do.

In a recent professional development session I facilitated, a teacher announced, "I cannot afford to keep buying bags of candy to get my kids to do their work." Although the candy initially worked well as a motivator, the teacher was now in a situation where she had to provide a steady stream of sweets, or students would stop working. If this teacher had instead helped her students develop internal self-efficacy with inspired classroom practices and engaging lessons, her learners would have been much more motivated. This is not to say that we can never do nice things for our kids; an occasional popcorn party can make school more fun. Just don't expect it to yield a long-term "pop" in motivation and achievement.

Reflections on Student Motivation

Student motivation does not just happen; teachers need to make a conscious effort to build and sustain it. Uninspired lessons do not yield inspired learners. What motivates kids may seem counterintuitive in some ways: bribes and rewards, while happily accepted by students, do not work as well as compelling, relevant tasks given in a positive, encouraging environment. These two pieces—the tasks and the instructional setting—are what spark students' motivation to work.

For struggling learners who are on the cusp of withdrawing from the learning community, these factors are particularly important. They need riveting tasks to pull them back in to the academic world. And, because their answer to the crucial question "Can I do this?" may initially be a resounding *no,* we must ensure that we provide a welcoming environment that enhances their self-efficacy and enables them to reach their potential.

Experiencing academic difficulty the previous year (or the previous period) does not condemn students to a life sentence of weak academic performance, but *they* must believe that as much as we do. Fortunately, we can embed challenging, supportive, inspiring strategies into every lesson. The more genuine optimism we show about students' potential for success, the more positive they will feel about their prospects—and the better they will perform.

Checklist for student motivation:

Task construction:

❏ Tasks have high relevance and value.

❏ Tasks have an appropriate level of challenge: achievable without sacrificing rigor.

❏ Tasks are differentiated when appropriate.

❏ Tasks incorporate social interactions.

❏ Tasks are of appropriate duration.

Learning environment:

❏ Student recognition is genuine and deserved.

❏ Mistakes are considered part of learning, not cause for embarrassment.

❏ Teacher sets short-term goals for students.

❏ Grouping is strategic and cultivates success for all.

❏ Supplies are made available without shame.

❏ Teacher reactions are dependable and calm.

❏ Students have appropriate autonomy over learning.

❏ Feedback is ongoing and productive.

❏ Teacher makes routine personal connections with students.

8

Scaffolding: Providing What's Missing Just in Time

A frustrated piano student learning a new piece of music struggles to find the right tempo. Observing this, her teacher sets a metronome to the correct number of beats per minute. As the pianist practices, the tick, tick, tick of the pendulum guides her practice. As the student makes progress, she stops using the metronome for all but the most difficult passages. Once she masters those, use of the metronome ceases altogether. To help the student access higher rigor, this teacher made a decision to employ scaffolding. Together, the teacher and learner decided when the scaffolding should fade or cease entirely.

A different type of scaffolding is evident on youth baseball fields. For the youngest players, hitting a pitched ball would be practically impossible. Instead, the coach places a softer ball on a tee and adjusts the stand's height for each batter. As batters gain more confidence and success, they have the option of trying to hit a pitched ball. If a batter is unable to hit the pitched ball after a few attempts, he can return to hitting it off the tee. As players make progress, the stand is used less. Before long, every player will be able to hit a pitched ball. To help students reach the rigorous goal of hitting a pitched ball, the coach bridged the gap between their current ability and the skill they aimed for. As players individually showed progress toward the goal, the use of scaffolding diminished.

In a math classroom, students are adding numbers with decimals. The teacher observes that a few students would benefit from additional support in keeping the numbers aligned properly. She models a strategy of drawing lines on the paper to keep the numbers straight and thinks aloud for students as she demonstrates the placement of the decimals. Students draw the lines on their paper and practice using this approach. As some students get feedback on their proper use of the process and start getting more correct answers, they use the lines less frequently; other students continue the practice as needed.

Why Scaffolding Works

Introduced by Wood, Bruner, and Ross (1976), *scaffolding* is a process used to help learners perform tasks that would be too difficult for them to complete without assistance. On a construction site, scaffolding enables workers to reach otherwise inaccessible high points, such as a rooftop. In the classroom, the "rooftop" is the rigor of the standard, and scaffolding consists of supports or strategies that enable students to reach higher—to achieve more—than they could without it. With scaffolding, students can perform on a higher plane because their thoughts are not clouded with confusion over every missing skill, vocabulary word, or concept. An absence of scaffolding can result in continued miscues, frustration, and failure.

Scaffolding allows struggling students to reach up to the next level. Rather than being penalized for something they did not get in 1st, 3rd, or 6th grade, students get the information they need to do the academic job that is in front of them right now. Can't recall tricky verb conjugations? Here's a bookmark with that information. Having trouble simplifying fractions? Use this explanatory flowchart. Running across unfamiliar vocabulary words that hamper understanding? The text has been annotated with synonyms in the margins. Can't remember the order of operations? Here's a goofy mnemonic device to remind you.

Scaffolding enables instruction to move forward and backward at the same time. It fills in past gaps in the context of today's learning. It also looks forward to challenges in the new learning that may need to be bridged. For students who need an extra boost to get the hang of new concepts, scaffolding can be an academic lifesaver.

Vygotsky (1978) observed that students have two "levels." One level is where they are now, where they can work independently. The second level is their potential development, which is a stretch beyond their current academic position. This zone of proximal development is where learning is bridged with support from teachers and peers. Because scaffolding is about helping students reach their potential, all students can benefit from scaffolding at certain critical junctures.

Scaffolding helps students in all content areas. Belland, Walker, Olsen, and Leary (2012) determined that scaffolding positively affects student learning in STEM areas across all grade levels, from kindergarten through high school graduation. Their results showed that scaffolding has a significant effect size of 0.53. In addition, Magno (2010) found that students who received scaffolding during reading showed significant improvement in speed and oral proficiency and even experienced a marked decrease in anxiety during reading.

Some may argue that scaffolding leads to too much dependence on supportive devices or strategies. Properly executed, however, scaffolding fosters student self-reliance. A simple bookmark listing capitalization rules, a sample of a problem correctly done, or a flowchart showing the steps of an investigative process gives students exactly what they need to accomplish the task in front of them. Without them, the teacher would likely face a multitude of raised hands, or, worse, confused students might just give up in frustration. With scaffolds in place, students can continue with their work and handle missing pieces largely on their own.

Implementing Scaffolding

The purpose of scaffolding is to help students access the rigor of today's standard. Much scaffolding can be planned before the lesson begins. After creating standards walls and identifying key vocabulary, teachers should look backward and identify the prerequisite skills students need for mastery. From that list, they can create scaffolding devices, such as cheat sheets, graphic organizers, checklists, and bookmarks. If a standard has a prerequisite skill of working with negative numbers, for example, the teacher can create number lines for students to consult.

Next, teachers should look forward and identify difficult spots or common misconceptions students have about the new standard and plan for those situations, asking themselves, "What new concepts will be more readily attainable with bridges in place?" For example, a teacher could construct an anchor chart listing the parts of a paragraph or critical physics formulas. The bridges or scaffolds fade away as students no longer require them, but new ones may need to be constructed for the next learning goal.

Assessing each student's "actual" prior knowledge and zone of proximal development requires careful thought and ongoing observation and diagnosis. Students' understanding changes constantly, so the amount of scaffolding they receive should be adjusted as needed. Conducting ongoing observations will help teachers know when to provide additional scaffolding or tweak current scaffolds. Some good indicators of problem situations are persistent student questions or misconceptions on a topic or our own continued reiteration of certain points. For example, in a classroom I was in recently, students could not recall the multiple steps of a calculator function in the correct order. (Actually, there were too many steps for me to retain, either.) Rather than simply repeating "Scroll down, click here, now go here . . . ," a more effective approach would have been to stop and create a flowchart or write out simple steps for students. A lack of scaffolding devices can result in our minds getting bogged down in details rather than focusing on the central concept.

The question of when to reduce scaffolding is an important one. Although the goal is student independence, timing can vary by student and concept. Belland and colleagues (2012) found that a group whose scaffolding faded on a fixed schedule did not do as well as other students whose scaffolding faded according to ongoing observation. Systematically reducing scaffolding requires professional judgment based on observation and feedback.

Strategies for Scaffolding

To rein in the sweeping scope of scaffolding, it may be helpful to divide the approach into two categories: devices and strategies (see Figure 8.1).

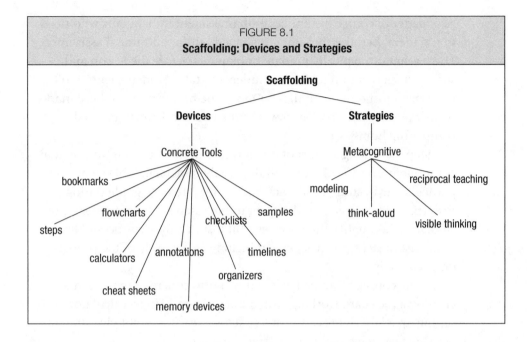

FIGURE 8.1
Scaffolding: Devices and Strategies

Instructional scaffolding devices are tangible tools that teachers put in students' hands, tape on desks or walls, or attach to pages in books. Teachers or students can create these devices. Scaffolding strategies, like modeling and reciprocal teaching, tend to be metacognitive in nature. Both types of scaffolding fade gradually, as students assume greater independence.

Scaffolding Devices

Teachers can provide the following scaffolding devices to students (or have students create them) to facilitate access to the standard. These are inserted just in time for new learning.

Bookmarks. Bookmarks are perfect for scaffolding students' knowledge of items that rely on memory. Capitalization rules, math and science formulas, parts of speech, perfect squares, punctuation rules, parts of cells, spelling rules, integer rules, prefixes and suffixes—the lists of things we expect students to remember is practically endless.

Bookmarks are incredibly versatile tools, and they are my favorite device. They are easy to create and use, unobtrusive, and safe, especially when they are offered to everyone. Providing broad access to this support as a matter of course minimizes embarrassment for students who need to use them, because they are not singled out for additional assistance. The teacher can typically prepare bookmarks before the lesson and simply stack them on tables for students to take. Students who don't need them just don't grab them. One of the best features of bookmarks is their portability: they can travel home with students to be used in completing homework.

Steps. Breaking a concept down into digestible parts is an essential component of scaffolding. Providing easily understandable steps, in particular, gives students a quick and useful reference guide during practice. Trimming verbiage and getting to the essence of a process supports students who might otherwise get a bit lost in a messy process. Next to the list of steps, the teacher can include an example of the process done correctly.

Many concepts can be broken down into concrete steps, such as creating a pie chart, working with a microscope, using a calculator, or setting up a lab. Here is a list of five steps a teacher might give students who are learning to solve a one-step equation:

1. Locate the variable.
2. Identify the operation.
3. Do the inverse.
4. Solve.
5. Check by substitution.

Flowcharts. Flowcharts show processes laid out in a systematic fashion, streamlining bulky information for easier interpretation and application. Flowcharts lend themselves well to concepts and processes like how a bill becomes a law, circuitry, causes of wars, steps in writing a research paper, economic events, and the scientific method (see Figure 8.2). Math concepts can also be effectively sequenced in flowcharts. Flowcharts' concise wording and visual presentation combine to make complex concepts more comprehensible.

Cheat sheets. Written on sticky notes or quarter-sheets of paper, cheat sheets, reminders, or shortcuts can lessen students' frustration and increase their perseverance on a task. Cheat sheets can provide scaffolding for a plethora of prerequisite skills or memory items, including

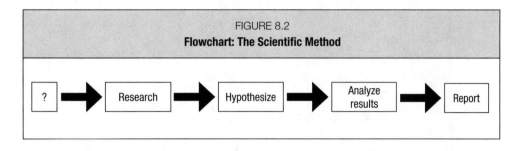

FIGURE 8.2
Flowchart: The Scientific Method

? → Research → Hypothesize → Analyze results → Report

- Irregular verbs.
- Inverse operations.
- Branches of government.
- Literary devices.
- Spelling or punctuation rules.
- The metric system.
- Types of rocks.
- Order of operations.

For example, students often have difficulty recalling integer rules when completing multiplication and division problems. They might complete all of their homework only to discover the next day that they used the incorrect signs. But if they follow the simple tic-tac-toe guide in Figure 8.3 (p. 140), all the signs will be perfect.

Although teachers can easily make and distribute cheat sheets and reminders, they should also encourage students to create their own customized ones. As adults, we frequently jot down reminders on sticky notes, and we can show students this way of scaffolding their own learning as well. Imagine being in a classroom where students routinely say things like "Let me make a reminder of that and put it in my book!"

Annotation. Annotating text provides an avenue for students to read challenging texts that include unfamiliar words, rather than reading in place. Teachers can provide explanations, synonyms, examples, and reminders in the margins of texts to assist with comprehension. Annotations work well in all content areas, including math. For example, next to a word problem that asks students to find the circumference of a cymbal, the teacher can jot down a drawing or short explanation of the term

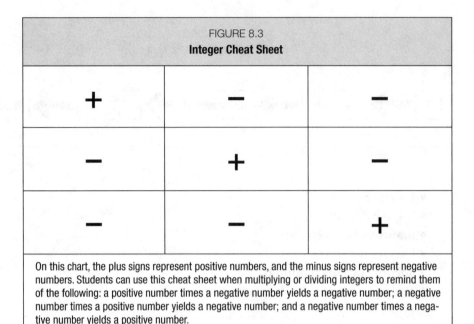

FIGURE 8.3
Integer Cheat Sheet

On this chart, the plus signs represent positive numbers, and the minus signs represent negative numbers. Students can use this cheat sheet when multiplying or dividing integers to remind them of the following: a positive number times a negative number yields a negative number; a negative number times a positive number yields a negative number; and a negative number times a negative number yields a positive number.

circumference as well as the word *cymbal,* which may be an unfamiliar incidental vocabulary term.

Depending on the lesson's structure, teachers can provide some students with annotated versions of texts and others not. When I set up reading stations, I provide multiple texts at varying reading levels and annotate some in advance, marking hints next to words that I have predicted may be unfamiliar to some students. For example, I may write, "starving!" next to *voracious* and "everywhere" next to *ubiquitous.* In addition, I signify degrees of importance, from "skip" to "very important." With independent textbook reading, individual students may have annotated versions (often containing explanatory sticky notes on challenging passages) that teachers can prepare in advance. Other times, the entire class may benefit from annotation directed by the teacher: "Let's all take a sticky flag and jot down this formula and stick it in the margin."

"Almost there" writing. Giving students a piece of writing that is "almost there" and asking them to complete it gives them an opportunity to develop their skills without confronting an ominous blank page.

With a bit of work on students' part, the text will be complete. Teachers can customize this device depending on their desired area of focus: for example, they can have students contribute topic sentences, closing thoughts, or supporting evidence. As students progress, the omissions they must fill in can become more significant. While some students may be given the task to write a paragraph about snails and their senses from scratch, others may benefit from completing the following "almost there" paragraph:

How Senses Help Snails Survive

Snails, which in the science world are known as gastropods, have developed senses that are critical to their survival. They have an organ that controls their balance. When a snail begins to get off balance, a signal _____.
In addition to a sense of balance, gastropods have sensitive smelling, or olfactory, organs. Consisting of four tentacles, these organs help snails smell by _____.
Their keen sense of smell is their most important sense because snails cannot hear and their sight is very weak. Because snails are mostly nocturnal, their eyesight is not as critical. They do have eyes, but most species can only distinguish between _____. These senses help snails survive as they avoid danger by _____.

Checklists and timelines. Students sometimes embark on large-scale projects with zeal but then get bogged down and never cross the finish line. They benefit from dividing large, long-term projects or papers into chunks or short-term goals. Reining in a larger process by providing smaller proximal goals not only scaffolds the process by giving students shorter periods of accountability but also builds more student ownership of the process. Teachers can develop these goals with students and revise them as needed. The following is an example of a checklist a teacher might provide to students working on a major research paper.

❑ Develop topic ideas (2/2)
❑ Determine audience (2/3)
❑ Gather resources and research (2/10)
❑ Create concept map (2/11)
❑ Complete first draft (2/15)
❑ Conference with teacher (2/16)
❑ Edit and revise (2/18)

Samples. Imagine assembling a piece of furniture with numerous parts without looking at the picture on the box. Sometimes, the most effective scaffolding is a sample of completed work. A math problem correctly worked, a well-constructed paragraph, or a completed project from the previous year gives students concrete examples of expectations. Samples take the nebulousness out of learning goals.

Even imperfect samples have value. For example, released writing papers from state exams help students understand varying degrees of proficiency. One caveat with samples is that students often have difficulty reading other students' handwriting. For that reason, I typically type or print handwritten student samples to show students.

Scaffolding Strategies

Metacognitive scaffolding strategies promote learners' awareness and development of their thought processes. We can help students monitor their learning by allowing them to peek into our thought processes and then transfer those models to their own processes. The following scaffolding strategies will build students' metacognitive skills in all content areas.

Think-alouds. Thinking aloud to students, particularly weaker readers, can help them monitor and improve specific reading comprehension skills (Davey, 1983). Students gain insight on the traits of good readers by hearing how others think during the reading process. As the teacher reads aloud a selected passage, she halts strategically to model thoughts that good readers tend to have. For example, when she comes to a heading, she may note, "I bet this part will be about. . . ."

During a think-aloud, the teacher can model such key reading skills as making predictions, questioning, and visualization. In addition, she can demonstrate "fix-it" strategies: "Gosh, I did not get that part—let me reread it. Oh, the picture gives me a clue." Thinking aloud is then transferred to students, who can read together in pairs and share their thinking.

Thinking aloud is not just for English class; it works in all content areas. For example, a math teacher could say, "I am thinking about how I can get this variable isolated. What operation would I need to do?"

Although think-alouds may have elementary school connotations, research (Edmonds et al., 2009) reveals that older students can also benefit from explicit reading comprehension strategies, although use of these strategies often diminishes as students move into the upper grades. The researchers found, however, that when interventions were continued, the group that reaped the highest gains was students with disabilities.

Reciprocal teaching. Reciprocal teaching uses teacher-student dialogue to show students how to use reading strategies like prediction, summarization, and questioning. Teachers first lead the process, modeling the traits of good readers by questioning, clarifying, and summarizing text as they read aloud. They gradually turn this process over to students, who transfer it to new text. Students now become the facilitators of this process, assuming the role of the teacher in leading discussions.

In a review of 16 studies on reciprocal teaching, Rosenshine and Meister (1994) found that students who engaged in reciprocal teaching scored higher than did the control group on both standardized and experimenter-developed comprehension tests. When the teacher taught explicit cognitive strategies before reading, the results were particularly strong. The teacher practices that were gradually relinquished to students included generating questions, summarizing, forming predictions, and clarifying confusing text. Encouragingly, below-average students showed significant improvement with this process. The tests administered to students used text that students had not seen before, indicating that students had successfully transferred these comprehension practices.

Annotation. Although teacher-annotated text given to students is a scaffolding device, teaching students to annotate on their own is a metacognitive strategy. When students begin to think about their reading and become aware of the words and concepts as opposed to just moving their eyes across the page, they are taking an important step in learner independence. It is important for teachers to model this process first, to walk students through the process of thinking about a text and making notes on it.

Visible thinking. When we walk into a classroom, what evidence of student thinking do we see? Student work may be posted on the walls, but what if it's days old? Students may be working silently for a substantial period, but what tangible proof do we have that they are getting it *right now*? What are they thinking about the concept at this moment? What are they *not* getting? If they are reading, how can we know the depth of their comprehension?

Visible thinking is exactly what it sounds like: student thinking made visible through active documentation. Visible thinking strategies have the power to pull students' thoughts from the shadows and bridge their achievement to a higher level. We have examined numerous visible thinking strategies throughout this book: students may make their thinking visible by annotating, coding, highlighting, or writing on sticky flags on a text, or by creating a chart that compares and contrasts two concepts, demonstrates cause and effect, or outlines a sequence of events.

In classrooms where thinking is visible, chart paper should be strewn around the room as students talk about their thinking and make notes with markers. Yes, it can be messy, because active thinking is messier than passive sitting.

When we are not able to see or hear the thinking of struggling students, we are putting them at greater risk of failure. Visible thinking keeps both students and teachers accountable: we cannot pretend that students are "getting it" or simply deliver information and hope for the best.

Reflections on Scaffolding

I sometimes liken a learner with knowledge and skill gaps to a ship with a few holes: it is our job to fix the holes while the ship continues to sail forward. To do otherwise denies some learners access to the rigor of the standards. We cannot allow learners to stop moving forward.

Scaffolding devices and strategies work in tandem to provide powerful support: while devices plug the gaps to enable students to continue to learn, strategies facilitate the thinking skills students need to learn new concepts. Both methods enable students to master tasks that are difficult but attainable with support.

Occasionally I encounter a teacher who thinks, "They can't learn *this* because they didn't get *that*." There is no doubt that learning is more frustrating and difficult for students with gaps. Without having committed basic skills to memory, it takes them longer to solve a math problem. Their writing has glaring deficiencies, and their reading levels make it difficult for them to get through dense informational reading. But if we just work on fixing students' flaws without simultaneously exploring new academic worlds, we'll succeed only in making school boring and miserable for lower-achieving students.

Scaffolding acknowledges that students do not remember every single thing that was ever taught. Strategic scaffolding for prerequisite and new skills has the power to move students upward, enabling them to grasp new concepts and achieve success. With these in place, students can learn today's lesson, even if they didn't get everything in the past.

Checklist for scaffolding:

❑ Scaffolding is based on ongoing observation and analysis.

❑ Prerequisite skills are identified prior to the lesson, and scaffolding is planned in advance.

❑ Scaffolding enables students to access the rigor of the standard.

❑ Scaffolding is tactically faded based on ongoing observation, formative assessment, and dialogue with students.

❑ Scaffolding is incorporated as a natural part of the learning process.

9

Why Are Some Students Still Failing, and What Can We Do About It?

Despite our best efforts, some students continue to fail. Academic failure in a broad sense consists of two elements. The first is what students bring to the learning environment: they may lack certain skills, complete homework assignments inconsistently, or exhibit low motivation. The other half of the equation is the school's response to student failure. Effectively countering failure requires first a correct diagnosis of its causes and then timely and steady interventions to reverse it.

For most of us, thinking about student failure conjures up pictures of students from past or current classrooms. The case of one particular 8th grader continues to haunt me, because her situation could easily have been fixed had we intervened earlier. This student was failing several classes, and her math and reading scores were below grade level, although she worked hard and completed her daily work. Her unit test scores hovered right around the passing mark, and her consistent daily grades kept her averages just above passing. The trouble was homework. More often than not, it was incomplete or substandard, which resulted in a string of zeros. At the parent-teacher conference, her mom was supportive and pledged to help in any way possible. She then confided, "I drive the morning bus run, so I leave the house when it's still dark. I park the bus during lunch and wait tables at a local restaurant. After that, I do my afternoon bus run and then return to the restaurant for the dinner shift. I typically get home around 10 o'clock. I talk to my daughter when I get breaks, and she tells me she is working on her homework."

Why was this student failing, and what would help solve the problem? On the surface, a good prescription might seem to be continuing to urge the girl to do her homework. But she was already trying to comply with teacher requests. She had the work ethic, the desire to do well, and adequate organizational skills. The student was *just* able to meet passing standards during the school day, when teachers were there to support and scaffold her efforts, but at home, she lacked the academic assistance to successfully complete most of the work. In addition, her weak reading and math skills made grade-level work an ongoing challenge.

What superficially appeared to be a willful refusal to do homework was actually a valiant but unsuccessful effort to accomplish something independently that was difficult enough with the help of highly trained teachers. Unfortunately, in this girl's case, missing homework grades combined with a woefully late and inadequate intervention resulted in grade-level retention. Her grade averages were too low to be salvageable, so she spent another year in 8th grade, repeating even the courses that she had passed.

This student's circumstances are typical of failing students. Although causes of failure vary by student, certain problems crop up repeatedly, including

1. Homework challenges.
2. Zeros or low grades given for missing work.
3. Lack of targeted, ongoing assessment and intervention.
4. Low student motivation.
5. Weak skills or knowledge gaps.

The following sections go into these problems in depth and provide guidance on how teachers can overcome persistent challenges and reverse students' downward trajectory.

Problem 1: Homework Challenges

My experience as a remedial education coordinator for a large school district put me on the front lines of student failure. Fruitless calls to administrators seeking ways to avoid grade retention all seemed to come down to the same complaint: students weren't doing their homework. One comment from a principal summed up teachers' frustration: "Teachers are not going to be receptive to your attempts to help this student avoid retention. They have been urging him to do his homework all year, and he has not complied. He should have done his work." In a way, this is an understandable position, but it highlights the thorny problem of at-risk students and homework.

Homework reaches outside the four walls of the classroom, moving learning to students' home environments, where they are largely on their own. Conditions conducive for learning, such as a quiet place to work and adequate supplies (including, these days, Internet access, office software, and a printer), are out of our control. Students may be babysitting their younger siblings or working at a job. Parents may lack the content knowledge to assist their children with assignments, or they may not even be home. For students who are academically hanging by a thread, the expectation that they must work at home with no assistance is problematic at best. At the very least, it will take these learners longer to complete homework than their more successful peers, and they will likely experience greater frustration—if they even try.

The next day, the whole class experiences the fallout resulting from last night's homework issues. Some students may have found it easy, while others struggled and have questions, and still others never got out of the gate. The teacher expends valuable class time addressing questions, while the students who got it are bored and the ones who did not even attempt it sink further.

Grading homework can exacerbate the problem. Some teachers give grades just for completion, so a student who has serious misconceptions but used a lot of ink may receive a perfect score while a student who completed just what she understood gets a 50, and the slew of students who didn't attempt the homework receive zeros. It is easy to understand why some teachers who work with high numbers of at-risk students simply give up on assigning homework.

So why put everyone through it? For one thing, research (Cooper, 1989) demonstrates a clear positive correlation between homework and achievement for secondary students. When two groups of high school students received the same instruction, but one group completed homework throughout the unit, the students who had completed homework outperformed 69 percent of the students who did not complete homework.

The positive effects were most pronounced with high school students, although junior high school students significantly benefited, too. Interestingly, there was little correlation between homework and achievement among 3rd–5th graders. Nevertheless, the author recommends giving younger children homework, but for different reasons, such as helping them develop good study habits.

In a more recent study analyzing research on homework from 1987 to 2003, Cooper, Robinson, and Patall (2006) found similar evidence that homework can have a positive influence on academic achievement. Again, gains were stronger in grades 7–12 than in grades K–6. Marzano and Pickering (2007) contend that the strong effect size of homework, which ranges, on average, from 0.21 to 0.88, makes it worth the effort and caution against dropping the practice. In their synthesis of homework research, they found that homework resulted in achievement gains ranging from 8 to 31 percentile points. Of course, students must actually *do* their homework to realize these gains. Therein lies the problem with struggling kids.

With the compelling evidence that homework can boost student achievement, it seems reasonable to routinely assign homework, particularly to secondary students. Tossing aside this instructional tool may diminish the gains made by the students who benefit from this practice. Students who *do* go home and complete their homework should not suffer academically on account of students who do not do it. On the other hand, students who are assigned homework that they simply cannot do without assistance should not be penalized with zeros.

Schools that are committed to extending learning at home should develop a proactive homework plan that addresses common issues and outlines the school's philosophy. Creating such a plan requires teachers and administrators to reflect on questions like "Why do we give homework in the first place?" and "What learning is so critical that family time, work time, playtime, and extracurricular events need to be set aside to accommodate the assignments?" Asking families to place homework as a top priority obliges us to provide them with clear goals and expectations. The following are some guidelines schools may want to incorporate into their homework plans:

• Homework's purpose and value will be clear, and it will help students master current standards.

• Teachers will publicly post assignments and include clear instructions using the school's communication channels (e.g., hotlines and websites).

• Homework will never be used as punishment (e.g., for behavior infractions).

• Students' grade level multiplied by 10 yields the maximum number of minutes that students should spend on homework each night (e.g., 7th graders will get no more than 70 minutes of homework). This is in keeping with recommendations from Cooper (1989).

• Students will be able to complete homework with minimal assistance from parents.

The guidelines a school develops go for all students, but a homework plan should also support learners with academic issues who may have difficulty doing the homework. If the building expectation is that homework is important to every student's success, then the school should take steps to ensure that every student completes his or her homework. Otherwise, homework may actually increase academic gaps between higher and lower achievers.

When we assign work in class, we provide a multitude of supports, including scaffolding, work samples, cooperative learning strategies, and feedback. It makes little sense, then, just to send struggling students off on their own to do homework with no teacher or peer support. One approach I have used with success is the "Lunch and Learn." Students who did not complete the assigned homework in my class were required to attend. For students who shared my lunch period, this was easy: we would eat together and knock out the homework. Another teacher would take my students who had different lunch periods, and I would take his or hers. The students didn't mind it at all; in fact, I think some enjoyed the additional interaction with teachers. Sometimes, they just needed structure; other times, they needed help understanding the assignment. Either way, the homework got done.

In another school, we implemented an "Opportunity Room," staffed by a rotation of teachers. Struggling students were assigned to go there, although any student could come voluntarily to work on homework. I was always surprised by the number of volunteer students, including athletes who wanted to get homework taken care of before a game. Schools are likely to have limited time to implement this program, but they can make use of homeroom or advisement periods, extended learning times, or connections/electives.

Principal David Guy and 6th grade science teacher Gary Garbe, both of Richland Middle School in Richland Center, Wisconsin, recognized their school's homework problem and came up with a solution (Garbe & Guy, 2006). They realized that each week, about 100 students (out of a student body of 330) either did not turn in their homework or turned it in late. The school's policy of deducting 10 percent off a student's homework grade each day the homework was late and mailing a letter to parents was not working. By the time the letter reached parents, the student's grade for the assignment was already decimated. Homework, the authors observed, was contributing to students' academic failure.

Looking for solutions, they surveyed students about why they were not doing their homework. Responses ranged from inadequate understanding of the assignment to distractions at home to lack of time. The school also surveyed parents and received a range of responses. Along with factors such as working late hours, parents shared that after a long day at work, they did not want to battle over homework and sometimes lacked understanding of the material.

In response to these findings, the school implemented a Learning Lab, held for an hour after school every day except Friday. The Learning Lab, administrators emphasized, was not punitive, but a place for learning. Staffed by teachers, administrators, and parents, the lab provided a place for students to get help on homework. Students who did not turn in a homework assignment were given the choice either to turn in the homework the next day or to attend the Learning Lab. Parents also had the option of sending their child to the lab. Another critical change the school made was notifying parents as soon as a problem came up, while there was still time for action.

Since the inception of the Learning Lab, Richland has documented a significant increase in homework completion, and teachers have given far fewer *F*s. In fact, the number of missing assignments each week has decreased by 76 percent. The school made the decision to support students with homework, and it has paid off.

Problem 2: Zeros for Missing Work

Reeves (2008) boldly stated that "the difference between failure and the honor roll often depends on the grading policies of the teacher" (p. 85). Of all detrimental grading practices, Reeves claims, giving zeros for missing work is the most toxic. As Richland Middle School staff recognized, students need to complete their work, not be punished with zeros.

A few zeros in the gradebook, especially for struggling students, can lead to student apathy and disengagement. Although the logic behind assigning zeros may be that it will "scare students straight"—that is, motivate them to work harder and complete their homework the next time—the reverse often ends up being the case. Once a student's grade point average is past saving, what's the point of working at all?

At the other end of this homework grading spectrum is the student who completes every assignment and receives a steady flow of 100s but barely passes the state-mandated tests at the end of the year. Her parents are left scratching their heads in disbelief: they were getting signals all year, via homework grades, that their daughter was at the top of the class.

Both these extremes illustrate the dangers of grading for completion only: grades should signal students' level of mastery of the standards, not how many (or how much) of their assignments they completed.

Teachers should also examine how they grade different types of homework. Student work improves with feedback, but not necessarily with grades. Schools sometimes have a misconception that everything students complete (or fail to complete) needs to have a grade attached to it. But if the homework functions as formative assessment—for example, if students are asked to complete practice problems or summarize a reading—then it doesn't make sense to grade it. These aren't the types of assignments that are typically graded during class, so why would they warrant a grade when they are completed at home? On the other hand, if the assignments are summative in nature—for example, longer-term culminating projects such as essays or a researched travel brochure—it makes sense to attach grades to them. Teachers will be able to address the homework grading conundrum more easily when they think of homework as an extension of the student work period.

Problem 3: Lack of Ongoing Assessment and Intervention

At the end of each semester or school year, schools are filled with a panicked flurry of activity. Students on the cusp of failure nervously await their fates. Teachers frantically grade final projects and papers. The academic version of *Let's Make a Deal* ensues: "What about bonus points for extra work?" or "I think I remember turning that paper in. . . ." Counselors' offices are packed with parents, and office voicemail systems exceed capacity. Complicated grading mechanisms calculate students' futures. Parents swear that this is the first they have heard about their child's possible retention, and administrators scramble for documentation of all the calls made throughout the year. An entire year of learning and assessment funnels into a few days of make-or-break decisions: will students pass or fail?

Ongoing assessment, intervention, and parent communication are essential in preventing student failure. When any student in the building is in danger of failing, the equivalent of tornado warning sirens should wail around the school. This is an emergency in this student's life, and the sirens should not cease until action has been taken to remedy the failure.

The National Dropout Prevention Center's (2013) policy statement on student grade retention (www.dropoutprevention.org/retention-policy) has six recommendations for grade retention, half of which relate to the urgency of ongoing assessment, intervention, and parent communication. A summary of these is as follows:

- All students must be periodically assessed to determine their progress.
- Students' schedules should allow for daily curricular interventions to meet their needs.
- Parents must be informed throughout the assessment and intervention process.

In addition to ongoing assessment, intervention, and communication, other remedies can help alleviate these springtime crises. One solution is to examine grades throughout the year on a schoolwide basis, homing in on low averages that are due to missing work or absences. Rather than leaving a zero in place, which can devastate a grade, teachers may consider reteaching the "problem" portion of the standard and giving students another opportunity to earn a passing grade. They could use the last hour of each week to reteach a concept to students who need it while other students embark on enrichment in a different part of the building. For some students, such timely second chances may be the difference between passing and failing.

In addition to giving students a second chance to master concepts, the ongoing use of portfolios throughout the year can be instrumental in telling a student's academic story over an extended period. Organized by learning goal, this is a systematic approach to examining work throughout the year (rather than over the course of a few days in the spring). Portfolios provide rich avenues for conversations about the standards with students and parents. Evidence of learning and progress is apparent, as are areas in need of growth, which teachers can address by reteaching material or providing additional practice.

Teachers should also reflect on the potential effect that large-scale, long-term projects with high grading weights have on final grades. Reeves (2008) has identified such projects as a common cause of failing grades. These can sink students at any time of the year but are particularly devastating at the end of a semester or school year, when there is no opportunity to fix the failure. Gathering ongoing evidence of learning in smaller chunks provides students with more frequent and manageable opportunities for demonstrating understanding or the lack thereof—and for addressing gaps while there is still time to make a difference.

Problem 4: Low Student Motivation

Getting to the root of why students are withdrawing from tasks and expending inadequate levels of effort takes some work and reflection. Every student wants to be successful, so it can be difficult to understand how a student can just sit there and not engage. Simply asking, "Why aren't you working harder?" can yield pat, superficial responses. "Class is boring" may actually mean, "The reading is too difficult for me." On the other hand, class may actually lack relevance and indeed be boring. If a student who doesn't make an effort in class works hard on the baseball field or in an after-school job, is the problem really a work ethic issue? It may be low self-efficacy. The student may be frozen academically— afraid to jump in and risk more failure. Alternatively, the task may be too difficult or too easy. Of course, sometimes the most obvious answer is correct: the student may in fact have developed poor work habits.

A good starting point in navigating the tricky business of diagnosing failure issues is to survey students. Although surveys provide just one piece of the bigger picture needed to understand what leads to failure, they can help pinpoint what is actually happening with students. Surveys can be used to simply and quickly assess a lesson's interest or difficulty level—for example, "With 1 being 'I can barely stay awake' and 5 being 'highly riveting,' assign a number to today's lesson" or "With 1 being 'way too easy' and 5 being 'way too hard,' assign a number to the task today." This survey can also use a multiple-choice format:

In math class today, the task we have been doing is:

❏ Too easy for me.
❏ About the right degree of difficulty.
❏ Too difficult.

To get more specific feedback, teachers can ask students to complete a prompt:

What would help me be more successful in class is
_____.

What I would like for you to know about me as a learner is that
_____.

I would participate more in class if _____.

Fortunately, when the issue is low engagement or motivation, teachers can often address it with instructional strategies, including

• Incorporating individual learning styles into instruction and assignments.
  • Providing choices for greater learner autonomy.
  • Pairing less-engaged students with more-engaged students.
  • Increasing tasks' value and relevance.
  • Tweaking tasks' difficulty level.
  • Giving immediate, descriptive feedback.
  • Incorporating cooperative learning regularly.

Encouraging students to participate in extracurricular activities can also benefit those who are withdrawing from classroom participation. In a study (Mahoney, 2000) that followed 695 students from childhood through age 24, students involved in extracurricular activities were less likely to drop out, behaved better in class, and were even less likely to get arrested than students who weren't involved. Interestingly, the positive effects of these activities persisted past students' school days and most strongly benefited students who were at the highest risk of committing antisocial behavior. The improvement was partially credited to the increased connection students shared with faculty members and peers. Not just any extracurricular activity works, however: the study found that four criteria contribute to an activity's success, including (1) a highly organized structure; (2) regular meetings; (3) skill-building to reach common goals; and (4) competent adult leadership.

In the vein of developing connections with students, Mendler (2000) recommends a strategy called the "two-by-ten intervention": for two undivided minutes each day, for 10 consecutive days, a teacher talks with an unmotivated student about anything *except* the student's poor academic situation. These interactions may take place between classes, during lunch, at the lockers, during bus duty, or in the classroom. Topics may range from sports to music to television shows—anything to build connectivity with the student. Mendler claims that by the end of the 10th interaction, student work completion increases.

A similar approach used by one elementary administrator with whom I worked is TLC (Tender Loving Care). Any teacher in the building could signal a TLC alert that let teachers and administrators know that a certain student was having a tough day. Everyone in the building then gave that student a little extra positive attention just at the right time.

A practice that worked well for me, with the same goal of connectivity, is "Teacher's Pet of the Week." Anyone who has taught middle grades has witnessed students' preoccupation with fairness. "He passed out papers yesterday!" "Why does she always get to take the attendance changes to the office?" Students at this age appear to have a built-in barometer of equality, and they are particularly sensitive to perceptions of classroom favorites. For Teacher's Pet of the Week, which is completely voluntary, students enter their names in a jar for the weekly drawing. Throughout the year, everyone who wants to gets a turn at being the pet of the week. During his or her week, the pet student runs errands, lines up first for lunch, and so on. In addition, I awarded the pets their favorite candy bar and just doted on them all week. Although there is not a shred of evidence to support this approach, my kids loved it. The practice also made me aware that sometimes I was guilty of repeatedly choosing certain students I knew were reliable and inadvertently skipping over others.

Problem 5: Weak Skills or Knowledge Gaps

Students who continue to persevere despite setbacks and obstacles deserve our admiration. If they continue to have trouble despite putting in hard work, however, the problem may be academic and not entirely in their power to fix. One of the most common reasons for failure is reading challenges. The good news is that there are solutions to reading problems, both in the classroom and in out-of-school time (OST) programs.

In a study by Lauer and colleagues (2006), at-risk students who attended OST programs showed more improvement than those who did not participate. One of the strongest effects was in reading, particularly for early elementary and high school students. The model showing the highest gains was one-on-one tutoring.

Slavin, Karweit, and Waski (1992) also found one-on-one tutoring to be effective in reading and urged schools to do everything possible to remedy reading problems in the early grades. They assert that early reading problems can lead to sustained negative consequences, including students spending their entire school careers in special education.

A synthesis (Wanzek et al., 2013) of 19 studies of reading interventions with students after 3rd grade found that although gaining traction in reading is easier for younger students, adolescents can also improve their reading with appropriate interventions. These results not only confirm the imperative nature of early-grades reading intervention but also suggest the importance of continuing these interventions for older students. Schools need to do everything they can to fix reading problems early, but secondary schools must continue to work to improve students' reading skills.

During content-area classes, reading is more often about survival than enjoyment. Students need to be able to comprehend passages well enough to successfully complete a task or goal; those who read below grade level encounter hurdles to success with every assigned reading. The nature of informational text brings special challenges: textbooks are essentially dry reference materials filled with often-unfamiliar vocabulary. Within the content-area reading environment, however, several strategies can help students grasp the content while developing their reading skills. For example, teachers could

• Begin every reading with a pre-reading activity that piques interest and taps into prior knowledge, such as looking at content-related pictures or brainstorming.

• Preview essential vocabulary words that students will encounter in the reading.

• Provide choices in reading. (Even within the language arts classroom, there is little reason for every student to read the same novel. Teachers might try incorporating literature circles with a variety of reading choices to stimulate interest and engage varying reading levels.)

• Provide shorter passages containing just the critical content to lessen frustration and increase comprehension.

• Annotate passages with synonyms of critical vocabulary.

• Use during-reading strategies for all informational readings, such as sticky notes and annotation.

• Use leveled passages during cooperative learning activities and at stations.

- Incorporate multiple sources of text besides the textbook.
- Use paired readings in which both partners have specific jobs to do.
- Incorporate audio or video snippets to plug holes in understanding.

Because much of content understanding develops through reading, every teacher is, in effect, a reading teacher. Although a reading specialist may be the one designated to provide one-on-one tutoring, students are in content-area classes much of the day. The bulk of effective reading practices, then, must fall on the shoulders of every teacher.

In math, the cause of student failure may be a lack of understanding of the new concept, calculation errors resulting from missing prerequisite skills, or both. Teachers can address gaps in basic skills with scaffolding devices, such as bookmarks or cheat sheets, often taped to desks as a reference. Although it is obviously more desirable for students to have these facts committed to memory, new concepts must not be sacrificed because of these missing pieces. To assist students in understanding concepts the first time through, teachers should also make sure to

- Clearly articulate learning goals.
- Break down concepts into steps.
- Give students samples of correctly executed work to consult.
- Pair struggling students with more knowledgeable partners.
- Incorporate cooperative learning activities.
- Provide immediate feedback, particularly during the early stages of new learning, when errors tend to be more frequent.
- Offer choices or multiple avenues for students to demonstrate understanding.
- Illustrate concepts with concrete representations.
- Assign fewer problems at a time to allow opportunities for feedback before students practice on their own.

Retention Versus Promotion: What to Do When Students Fail

Let's say a school has attempted seemingly every research-based strategy and intervention throughout the year. Teachers have routinely articulated explicit learning goals, scaffolded prerequisite skills, integrated ongoing vocabulary development within relevant tasks, and employed strategies to increase student efficacy. The school has introduced acceleration and tutoring programs and given all students the opportunity to complete their homework with a professional educator's assistance. Yet at the end of the year, there are still students who have not met the minimum requirements to pass.

Two bad choices remain: retention or promotion. In an attempt to promote accountability, the perception of rigor, and the notion that students will "catch up" next year, the school may choose grade-level retention as the better option. Retention may at least seem better than promotion, which means knowingly moving students with major learning gaps to the next grade. The logic is that students will better understand the concepts the second time through.

However, research is decidedly and persuasively against retaining students in grade, which is often the course of last resort. In their review of 17 studies on retention, Jimerson, Anderson, and Whipple (2002) found that grade retention is one of the most prevalent predictors of dropout. Further, retaining students had no more positive academic impact than promoting them to the next grade. Rather than improving students' academic achievement, retention increased their odds of dropping out.

Evidence shows that retention in lower grades can harm students, too. Silberglitt, Jimerson, Burns, and Appleton (2006) debunked the common myth that retaining students in the early years somehow prevents failure in later grades. Although students may make short-term academic gains, these are potentially at the expense of academic failure and dropout down the road. According to Jimerson (2001), research stands so solidly against retention that the conversation needs to focus less on whether to promote or retain students than on finding productive interventions that prevent the need to take either course of action.

In sum, retention is not an intervention for academic achievement and in fact can exacerbate the negative effects of failure. If it's too late for intervention and the choice comes down to retention or promotion, promotion at least offers some hope for academic redemption.

Putting It All Together: Case Studies from Three Schools

In this book, I have presented eight powerful approaches that can be seamlessly interwoven in the classroom to help struggling students reach their potential. Implemented with consistency and fidelity, these practices get at the root of many academic problems.

Students who are underperforming likely have gaps in prior knowledge, vocabulary, and basic skills. They may have started defining their world in pessimistic terms and lost motivation to put forth any effort. Their academic hope may have diminished, and they may exhibit self-protection behaviors that sabotage their own learning. These eight instructional tactics proactively address issues that lead to failure by systematically moving struggling students forward, with support.

The following three schools graciously agreed to share the results they attained from implementing the approaches discussed throughout this book. Math was a particular focus for these schools. Teachers received professional development in creating standards walls, using scaffolding techniques, developing students' vocabularies, conducting formative assessment, implementing acceleration, integrating student work period practices, using success starters, and building students' self-efficacy. Throughout the process, building leaders provided teachers with classroom support and follow-up.

Common new features in these schools included standards walls that established clear learning goals, acceleration classes for students with identified gaps, TIP charts, scaffolding, cooperative learning, and a strong emphasis on visible learning for immediate feedback. All students' achievement improved significantly, and students with disabilities showed particularly impressive gains. Figure 9.1 (p. 162) breaks down each school's results in further detail.

Burney-Harris-Lyons Middle School

The teachers at Burney-Harris-Lyons understand that building confident learners requires more than telling kids, "You can do it!" Students who need additional support in math or language arts participate in a 55-minute acceleration class first thing in the morning called Extended Learning Time (ELT). Principal Melanie Sigler is a big believer in acceleration: "Students have so much more confidence now and know what to expect in class. I would highly recommend acceleration to schools; it has been phenomenal for our kids." In fact, she credits the school's shift from a remedial framework to an acceleration approach as a major factor

FIGURE 9.1 Results for Three Middle Schools		
School	**Demographics**	**Results**
Burney-Harris-Lyons Middle School (Grades 6–8), Athens, GA	• 598 students • 83 percent eligible for free or reduced-price lunch • Student population (rounded): 54 percent African American 33 percent Hispanic 10 percent Caucasian 3 percent multiracial	From 2010–2011 to 2011–2012, mathematics achievement increased 6 percent for student body as a whole and 7.2 percent for students with disabilities.
Clarke Middle School (Grades 6–8), Athens, GA	• 601 students • 65 percent eligible for free or reduced-price lunch • Student population (rounded): 54 percent African American 28 percent Caucasian 11 percent Hispanic 4 percent multiracial 3 percent other	From 2010–2011 to 2011–2012, mathematics achievement increased 7.9 percent for student body as a whole and 14.8 percent for students with disabilities.
Claxton Middle School (Grades 6–8), Claxton, GA	• 361 students • 81 percent eligible for free or reduced-price lunch • Student population (rounded): 43 percent Caucasian 37 percent African American 17 percent Hispanic 3 percent other	From 2009–2010 to 2010–2011, mathematics achievement increased 5.6 percent for student body as a whole and 40.7 percent for students with disabilities.

in its uptick in student achievement scores. She has found it particularly powerful for students in special education.

Ms. Sigler and her teachers make instructional decisions based on observations and data. Students are not locked into an Extended Learning Time track. When students improve and want to move from the acceleration ELT class to the enrichment ELT class to further extend their learning, administrators, teachers, and students collaborate on reaching those decisions. What has most surprised the staff is the value students themselves place on acceleration. Two 8th grade students requested to be moved into math acceleration after they observed their friends' improvement. Another student, who had progressed to the point of being scheduled *out* of acceleration, wrote a letter asking to stay put. She did not want to jeopardize her progress.

Ms. Sigler also credits the proximal goals and support provided by standards walls and TIP charts as confidence builders: "The standards can seem so overwhelming to kids, but this visual roadmap allows them to see the big picture. When they move the arrow and see their mastery and progress, I can see the confidence in our students. They are like, 'Wow! This looked like a lot, but look what we've done!'"

Clarke Middle School

Tad MacMillan, the principal of Clarke Middle School, characterizes his school's use of TIPs as "huge." In his view, TIPs have become the cornerstone of vocabulary instruction at Clarke. Teachers do not direct students to copy definitions from the dictionary; instead, they have students manipulate words, create illustrations, and develop nonexamples. Students keep their own TIPs in their interactive notebooks, too. As MacMillan puts it, "We're not just teaching the vocabulary; we're teaching students how we *learn* vocabulary." Peeking into the school's classrooms, it is common to hear students and teachers alike say, "Hey, that word should be on our TIP!"

Claxton Middle School

Claxton Middle School's shift from simply posting standards to using standards walls demonstrates the benefit that all students, particularly those who struggle academically, derive from explicit, graphically supported instruction.

When Claxton teachers began implementing standards walls, they noticed a change in their students. Ms. Threattle, a math instructional leader who works with all grade levels, realized that transforming long-winded standards into a clear standards wall was working when one of her students piped, "So this is showing us where we're going—like a map. I know if we're going all the way to Savannah or just to the park." In Ms. Threattle's words, "The standards walls serve as a filter. Learners can see what is most important today, but they also get a glimpse of the future." The standards walls are continually referred to throughout the day, and students gain an awareness of the progress they are making.

Because Claxton also has an acceleration program, Ms. Threattle was able to see firsthand the power of introducing standards walls and vocabulary to acceleration students before covering the material in the core class. Students let her know they had more confidence in class, especially once they had a stronger grasp on vocabulary. She recalls, "We saw student anxiety decrease and confidence swing upward. It was as if students were thinking, 'Hey, I know a little bit about this, so I can relax and focus on learning.' "

Standards walls don't just work for students; they can serve as an invaluable planning tool for teachers as well. As Ms. Threattle observes, "They make everyone think about the standards more clearly. We think about prerequisites and gather what we need to teach more effectively."

Reflections on Learning in the Fast Lane

The richest opportunities for students to succeed happen during their first time through a grade or course. Accordingly, schools should avail themselves of every conceivable research-based strategy they can to prevent failure, because after failure takes hold of a child, things are decidedly tougher. The most inspired instruction on earth can fall flat with a student who has already given up hope. In a leadership meeting I recently attended, a frustrated high school administrator asked, "How many times are we required to schedule the same students for the same classes? Their grades are actually going down on the second and third attempts instead of up. They are getting *worse* at the subjects." The cause of this slide was more likely student hopelessness than a decline in content knowledge.

We must make reflective instructional decisions on behalf of our students who are at risk of failing. These students need and deserve the most effective, high-impact practices we can implement. To give them any less risks widening achievement gaps.

In a school that uses these best practices, students may begin the day in an acceleration class that primes them for learning with just enough knowledge to spark connections in their regular class. The first minutes of every class bring immediate success with an engaging, powerhouse opener. The student work period is rich with cooperative interaction and student autonomy. Teachers provide minute-by-minute assessment and feedback so that students who experience momentary downward spirals get caught before they fall too far. Teachers fill in missing pieces from past grades, integrate academic vocabulary contextually and provide multiple exposures to new words, and buoy students' self-efficacy by weaving motivational strategies into lessons.

Using these practices consistently and pervasively brings to students our most effective instructional game, which is what is required to turn around academically weak or demotivated learners. Providing these frequent opportunities for small successes ignites students' desire for more success, deepens perseverance, and keeps them open to learning and always gaining momentum. No matter what students' outward signals may indicate, they want to do well at school. For some, it may have been a while since they have seen evidence of academic promise. It is within our power to make the classroom a place of hope for them.

In many ways, building academic success with students at risk of failure is about doing the opposite of what we've always done. In place of passive basic-skills work, we deploy exciting hands-on tasks. Rather than working alone, struggling students collaborate with successful students who, in addition to understanding the content, demonstrate perseverance, determination, and academic optimism. Instead of remediating past gaps, we accelerate students' learning and keep them in the fast lane, where we can easily see their progress. Instead of opening class with bland reviews and warm-ups, we spark excitement and immediate success. In place of posting a murky standard, we wow students with learning progressions that enable them to see where they are going and how it connects to where they have been. Instead of handing out more and more grades, we provide richer and richer feedback.

These youngsters are the most frustratingly wonderful students to teach. They often arrive at school with gaps and attitudes, but seeing them succeed in the classroom is the most rewarding thing a teacher can experience. Thoughtful instruction that addresses underlying issues can save these students. And they are so worth saving.

References

Ames, C. (1992). Classrooms: Goals, structures, and student motivation. *Journal of Educational Psychology, 84*(3), 261–271.

Armbruster, B., Anderson, T., Armstrong, J., Wise, M., Janisch, C., & Meyer, L. (1991). Reading and questioning in content area lessons. *Journal of Reading Behavior, 23*(1), 35–59.

Ashcraft, M. H., & Kirk, E. P. (2001). The relationship among working memory, math anxiety, and performance. *Journal of Experimental Psychology, 130*(2), 224–237.

Bandura, A. (1984). Recycling misconceptions of perceived self-efficacy. *Cognitive Therapy and Research, 8*(3), 231–255.

Beck, I., McKeown, M., & Kucan, L. (2002). *Bringing words to life.* New York: Guilford Press.

Becker, W. (1977). Teaching reading and language to the disadvantaged—what we have learned from field research. *Harvard Educational Review, 47*(4), 518–543.

Belland, B., Walker, A., Olsen, M., & Leary, H. (2012). *Impact of scaffolding characteristics and study quality on learner outcomes in STEM.* Paper presented at the 2012 Annual Meeting of the American Educational Research Association, Vancouver, Canada.

Black, P., & Wiliam, D. (1998). Inside the black box: Raising standards through classroom assessment. *Phi Delta Kappan, 80*(2), 139–148.

Bomia, L., Beluzo, L., Demeester, D., Elander, K., Johnson, M., & Sheldon, B. (1997). *The impact of teaching strategies on intrinsic motivation.* (ERIC Document Reproduction Service No. ED 418925)

Brophy, J. (2010). *Motivating students to learn.* New York: Routledge.

Clymer, J., & Wiliam, D. (2007). Improving the way we grade science. *Educational Leadership, 64*(4), 36–42.

Cooper, H. (1989). Synthesis of research on homework: Grade level has a dramatic influence on homework's effectiveness. *Educational Leadership, 47*(3), 85–91.

Cooper, H., Robinson, J., & Patall, E. (2006). Does homework improve academic achievement? A synthesis of research, 1987–2003. *Review of Educational Research, 76*(1), 1–62.

Csikszentmihalyi, M. (1990). *Flow: The psychology of optimal experience.* New York: HarperCollins.

Davey, B. (1983). Think aloud: Modeling the cognitive processes of reading comprehension. *Journal of Reading, 27*(1), 44–47.

Davies, A. (2007). Involving students in the classroom assessment process. In D. Reeves (Ed.), *Ahead of the curve: The power of assessment to transform teaching and learning* (pp. 31–57). Bloomington, IN: Solution Tree.

Day, B., & Drake, K. (1986). Developmental and experiential programs: The key to quality education and care of young children. *Educational Leadership, 44*(3), 24–27.

Deci, E. L., Koestner, R., & Ryan, R. (2001). Extrinsic rewards and intrinsic motivation in education: Reconsidered once again. *Review of Educational Research, 71*(1), 1–27.

Dicintio, M. J., & Gee, S. (1999). Control is the key: Unlocking the motivation of at-risk students. *Psychology in the Schools, 36*(3), 231–237.

Edmonds, M., Vaughn, S., Wexler, J., Reutebuch, C., Cable, A., Klingler, K., et al. (2009). A synthesis of reading interventions and effects on reading comprehension outcomes for older struggling readers. *Review of Educational Research, 79*(1), 262–300.

Eldredge, J., Reutzel, D., & Hollingsworth, P. (1996). Comparing the effectiveness of two oral reading practices: Round-robin reading and the shared book experience. *Journal of Literacy Research, 28*(2), 201–225.

Garbe, G., & Guy, D. (2006, Summer). No homework left behind. *Educational Leadership, 63*. Available: www.ascd.org/publications/educational-leadership/summer06/vol63/num09/No-Homework-Left-Behind.aspx

Georgia Department of Education. (2012). *Georgia performance standards for social studies: American government/civics*. Atlanta, GA: Author. Retrieved from www.georgiastandards.org/standards/Georgia%20Performance%20Standards/American-Government.pdf

Gillies, R., & Ashman, A. (1998). Behavior and interactions of children in cooperative groups in lower and middle elementary grades. *Journal of Educational Psychology, 90*(4), 746–757.

Graves, M. F. (2006). *The vocabulary book: Learning and instruction*. New York: Teachers College Press.

Hansen, D. (1989). Lesson evading and lesson dissembling: Ego strategies in the classroom. *American Journal of Education, 97*(2), 184–208.

Harlen, W., & Crick, R. (2003). Testing and motivation for learning. *Assessment in Education, 10*(2), 169–207.

Hart, B., & Risley, T. R. (1995). *Meaningful differences in the everyday experiences of young American children*. Baltimore: Paul H. Brookes.

Harvey, S., & Goudvis, A. (2007). *Strategies that work: Teaching comprehension for understanding and engagement*. Portland, ME: Stenhouse Publishers.

Hattie, J., & Timperley, H. (2007). The power of feedback. *Review of Educational Research, 77*(1), 81–112.

Hawkins, D., Doueck, H., & Lishner, D. (1988). Changing teaching practices in mainstream classrooms to improve bonding and behavior of low achievers. *American Educational Research Journal, 25*, 31–50.

Hirsch, E. D., Jr. (2003, Spring). Reading comprehension requires knowledge of words and the world: Scientific insights into the fourth-grade slump and the nation's stagnant comprehension scores. *American Educator*, 10–29.

Hoy, A., & Davis, H. (2006). Teacher self-efficacy and its influence on the achievement of adolescents. In F. Pajares & T. Urdan (Eds.), *Self-efficacy beliefs of adolescents* (pp. 117–137). Greenwich, CT: Information Age Publishing.

Hoyt, L. (2009). *Revisit, reflect, retell: Time-tested strategies for teaching reading comprehension*. Portsmouth, NH: Heinemann.

Jenkins, J. R., Stein, M. L., & Wysocki, K. (1984). Learning vocabulary through reading. *American Educational Research Journal, 21*(4), 767–787.

Jensen, E. (2005). *Teaching with the brain in mind*. Alexandria, VA: ASCD.

Jimerson, S. (2001). Meta-analysis of grade retention research: Implications for practice in the 21st century. *School Psychology Review, 30*(3), 420–437.

Jimerson, S., Anderson, G., & Whipple, A. (2002). Winning the battle and losing the war: Examining the relation between grade retention and dropping out of high school. *Psychology in the Schools, 39*(4), 441–457.

Johnson, D., & Johnson, R. (2009). An educational psychology success story: Social interdependence theory and cooperative learning. *Educational Researcher, 38*, 365–379.

Johnson, D., Maruyama, G., Johnson, R., Nelson, D., & Skon, L. (1981). Effects of cooperative, competitive, and individualistic goal structures on achievement: A meta-analysis. *Psychological Bulletin, 89*(1), 47–62.

Johnson, D., Skon, L., & Johnson, R. (1980). Effects of cooperative, competitive, and individualistic conditions on children's problem-solving performance. *American Educational Research Journal, 17*, 83–93.

Kagan, S., & Kagan, M. (2009). *Kagan cooperative learning*. San Clemente, CA: Kagan Publishing.

Lauer, P., Akiba, M., Wilkerson, S., Apthorp, H., Snow, D., & Martin-Glenn, M. (2006). Out-of-school-time programs: A meta-analysis of effects for at-risk students. *Review of Educational Research, 76*(2), 275–313.

Leahy, S., Lyon, C., Thompson, M., & Wiliam, D. (2005). Classroom assessment: Minute by minute, day by day. *Educational Leadership, 63*(3), 19–24.

Magno, C. (2010). The effect of scaffolding on children's reading speed, reading anxiety, and reading proficiency. *TESOL Journal, 3*, 92–98.

Mahoney, J. L. (2000). School activity extracurricular participation as a moderator in the development of antisocial patterns. *Child Development, 71*(2), 502–516.

Margolis, H., & McCabe, P. (2006). Improving self-efficacy and motivation: What to do, what to say. *Intervention in School and Clinic, 41*(4), 218–227.

Marzano, R. (2004). *Building background knowledge for academic achievement: Research on what works in schools*. Alexandria, VA: ASCD.

Marzano, R. (2007). Designing a comprehensive approach to classroom assessment. In D. Reeves (Ed.), *Ahead of the curve: The power of assessment to transform teaching and learning* (pp. 102–125). Bloomington, IN: Solution Tree.

Marzano, R., & Pickering, D. (2007). Special topic: The case for and against homework. *Educational Leadership, 64*(6), 74–79.

Marzano, R., Pickering, D., & Pollock, J. (2001). *Classroom instruction that works: Research-based strategies for increasing student achievement*. Alexandria, VA: ASCD.

Mendler, A. (2000). *Motivating students who don't care: Successful techniques for educators*. Bloomington, IN: Solution Tree.

Miller, D. (2009). *The book whisperer: Awakening the inner reader in every child*. San Francisco: Jossey-Bass.

Nagy, W. E., & Herman, P. A. (1984). *Limitations of vocabulary instruction*. Urbana, IL: University of Illinois, Center for the Study of Reading. (ERIC Document Reproduction Service No. ED 248498)

Nagy, W. E., & Townsend, D. (2012). Words as tools: Learning academic vocabulary as language acquisition. *Reading Research Quarterly, 47*(1), 91–108.

National Dropout Prevention Center. (2013). *NDPC policy statement on student grade retention.* Available: www.dropoutprevention.org/retention-policy

Pajares, F. (2006). Self-efficacy during childhood and adolescence: Implications for teachers and parents. In F. Pajares & T. Urdan (Eds.), *Self-efficacy beliefs of adolescents* (pp. 339–367). Greenwich, CT: Information Age Publishing.

Pearson, D., & Gallagher, M. (1983). *The instruction of reading comprehension* (Tech. rep. No. 297). Urbana, IL: University of Illinois at Urbana-Champaign, Center for the Study of Reading.

Pink, D. (2009). *Drive: The surprising truth about what motivates us.* New York: Riverhead Books.

Popham, W. J. (2008). *Transformative assessment.* Alexandria, VA: ASCD.

Powell, G. (1980). *A meta-analysis of the effects of "imposed" and "induced" imagery upon word recall.* Paper presented at the annual meeting of the National Reading Conference, San Diego, CA. (ERIC Document Reproduction Service No. ED 199644)

Protheroe, N. (2010, May/June). Boosting students' can-do attitude. *Principal,* 40–44.

Reeves, D. (2008). Leading to change: Effective grading practices. *Educational Leadership, 65*(6), 85–87.

Rosenshine, B., & Meister, C. (1994). Reciprocal teaching: A review of the research. *Review of Educational Research, 64*(4), 479–530.

Schunk, D. H., & Meece, J. L. (2006). Self-efficacy development in adolescence. In F. Pajares & T. Urdan (Eds.), *Self-efficacy beliefs of adolescents* (pp. 71–96). Greenwich, CT: Information Age Publishing.

Shearer, B., Ruddell, M., & Vogt, M. (2001). Successful middle school reading intervention: Negotiated strategies and individual choice. *National Reading Conference Yearbook, 50,* 558–571.

Shepard, L. (2000). The role of assessment in a learning culture. *Educational Researcher, 29*(7), 4–14.

Silberglitt, B., Jimerson, S., Burns, M., & Appleton, J. (2006). Does the timing of grade retention make a difference? Examining the effects of early versus later retention. *School Psychology Review, 35*(1), 134–141.

Slavin, R. (1983). When does cooperative learning increase student achievement? *Psychological Bulletin, 94*(3), 429–445.

Slavin, R. (1988, October). Cooperative learning and student achievement. *Educational Leadership, 46*(2), 31–33.

Slavin, R., Karweit, N., & Waski, B. (1992). Preventing early school failure: What works? *Educational Leadership, 50*(4), 10–18.

Sousa, D. (2008). *How the brain learns mathematics.* Thousand Oaks, CA: Corwin Press.

Sousa, D. A., & Tomlinson, C. A. (2011). *Differentiation and the brain: How neuroscience supports the learner-friendly classroom.* Bloomington, IN: Solution Tree Press.

Stahl, S. A., & Fairbanks, M. M. (1986). The effects of vocabulary instruction: A model-based meta-analysis. *Review of Educational Research, 56*(1), 72–110.

Stanovich, K. E. (1986). Matthew effects in reading: Some consequences of individual differences in the acquisition of literacy. *Reading Research Quarterly, 21*(4), 360–406.

Stiggins, R. (2004). New assessment beliefs for a new school mission. *Phi Delta Kappan, 36*(1), 22–27.

Stiggins, R. (2007). Assessment for learning: An essential foundation of productive instruction. In D. Reeves (Ed.), *Ahead of the curve: The power of assessment to transform teaching and learning* (pp. 58–76). Bloomington, IN: Solution Tree.

Stipek, D., & Weisz, J. (1981). Perceived personal control and academic achievement. *Review of Educational Research. 51*(1), 101–137.

Swanborn, M. S. L., & de Glopper, K. (1999). Incidental word learning while reading: A meta-analysis. *Review of Educational Research, 69*(3), 261–285.

Tankersley, K. (2005). *Literacy strategies for grades 4–12: Reinforcing the threads of reading.* Alexandria, VA: ASCD.

Usher, E., & Pajares, F. (2008). Sources of self-efficacy in school: Critical review of the literature and future directions. *Review of Educational Research, 78*(4), 751–796.

Vacca, R. T., & Vacca, J. A. L. (2002). *Content area reading: Literacy and learning across the curriculum.* Boston: Allyn and Bacon.

Vygotsky, L. (1978). *Mind in society: The development of higher psychological processes.* Cambridge, MA: Harvard University Press.

Wanzek, J., Vaughn, S., Scammacca, N., Metz, K., Murray, C., Roberts, G., et al. (2013). Extensive reading interventions for students with reading difficulties after grade 3. *Review of Educational Research, 83*(2), 163–195.

Westphal, L. (2009). *Differentiating instruction with menus.* Waco, TX: Prufrock Press.

Willis, J. (2006). *Research-based strategies to ignite student learning.* Alexandria, VA: ASCD.

Wood, D., Bruner, J., & Ross, G. (1976). The role of tutoring in problem solving. *Journal of Child Psychology and Psychiatry, 17,* 89–100.

Index

Note: Page references followed by an italicized *f* indicate information contained in figures.

171